"As a boxing historian I enjoy resear
fighters that are often overlooked ar
dues. Fighters from the Philippines
Some hardcore boxing fans may di
selections, but I nonetheless guara.
selected for this anthology."

>—Dan Cuoco, Director and Historian,
>International Boxing Research Organization

"Professors Gonzalez and Merino are two of the most gung-ho
observers of Philippine boxing that I know. That they are based
abroad makes them even more diligent in researching fact (and
fable) about Filipino and Filipina boxing legends. The stories
are fascinating and entertaining to read!"

>—Ed Picson, Executive Director,
>Amateur Boxing Association of the Philippines

"Gonzalez and Merino have produced an enjoyable one of a
kind sports memorabilia. The crisp biographies will knock you
out. A must read for all boxing fans!"

>—Joe Clough, Olympic gold medalist
>and three-time U.S. Best Boxing Coach

"This book is timely and enticing with the ascent of Manny
Pacquiao as the most popular boxer in the world. Culture and
sport have played an integral role in the lives of many Filipinos
and the San Francisco Bay Area has a rich tradition. Gonzalez
and Merino's research is long overdue and much of the
information may surprise many."

>—Bill Hogan, Director of Athletics,
>Seattle University, Washington

"These profiles and selections of Filipino Boxers are outstanding.
With current champion, Manny Pacquiao in the list, who wouldn't
be excited? As a long time trainer and spectator I enjoy the
rivalries between the Filipinos and Mexicanos. Great job!"

>—Candelario "Candy" Lopez, San Jose State University
>Head Coach and 2000 U.S. Olympic Boxing Coach

FROM PANCHO
TO PACQUIAO

FROM PANCHO TO PACQUIAO

Philippine Boxing In and Out of the Ring

JOAQUIN JAY GONZALEZ III
ANGELO MICHAEL F. MERINO

Mill City Press, Inc.

212 3rd Avenue North, Suite 290

Minneapolis, MN 55401

612.455.2294

www.millcitypublishing.com

ISBN-13: 978-1-937600-65-5

LCCN: 2012930108

Cover Photo by Ronnie Lu

Printed in the United States of America

TABLE OF CONTENTS

Preface

From Pancho to Pacquiao is a snapshot of more than a century of Philippine boxing.

It is a compilation of lucid and readable biographies of outstanding Philippine-born and Filipino American boxers, from Francisco "Pancho Villa" Guilledo to Manny "People's Champ" Pacquiao. Each story describes the rough roads these Filipino and Filipina boxers took to achieve fame and glory globally. It highlights not only their ring triumphs and disappointing losses but also the ups and downs of their lives outside professional boxing.

What makes this book unique is that every biography is situated in the context of the Philippine migration experience as well as the evolving history of boxing in the United States, in the Asian region, and globally. Classic and contemporary photos and our personal conversations combine to make the narratives real and vivid.

The journey to writing *From Pancho to Pacquiao: Philippine Boxing In and Out of the Ring* began with two individuals who shared a love and passion for teaching and boxing. During our many exchanges, both inside and outside of the ring, we joked about the possibility of co-teaching a formal Philippine boxing course. Inspired by the successes of Manny Pacquiao, what began as "What if" was transformed into "Let's do it!" Hence, together we crafted a university course,

"Philippine Boxing and Culture," which combined both boxing as a sport and an academic subject. After the formal college curriculum approval, we debuted the course in a room filled with 16 eager faces in Spring 2010.

The experiment proved to be a knockout. Our initial group of students spread the word throughout the University of San Francisco (USF) campus. The demand was so high that two sections had to be offered every semester. Eventually, building on the success of this sports and culture class, we developed a more social justice-oriented course, "Boxing and Social Justice," which was introduced in Fall 2011. Both courses were added as electives in the USF's Asian Studies Program and Yuchengco Philippine Studies Program. These are the first instances when Filipino-style boxing has been recognized as an academic subject outside of the Philippines.

In both Philippine boxing classes, we pieced together readily available materials we could find on this important but understudied subject. But since these were the only two courses of its kind in the globe, every time we taught, we always felt the burning desire to deviate from what was "readily available." This was a sign that we had to develop our own textbooks. *From Pancho to Pacquiao*, is one of these projects.

Nonetheless, *From Pancho to Pacquiao* is a book not just for our students but also for all who call themselves boxing aficionados and sports fans around the planet. Read on!

1

PANCHO VILLA

Kung walang tiyaga, walang nilaga.
(If you don't persevere, you get no reward.)

We believe that the story of Philippine boxing is as much the story of centuries of Filipino movement back and forth, from the Philippines and the United States.

A requirement for one of our politics and social justice classes at the University of San Francisco was a tour of historical landmarks that commemorate Filipino presence in the city. We would walk city streets named after Philippine heroes—Lapu Lapu, Bonifacio, Tandang Sora, Rizal, and Mabini. The tour would end at the San Lorenzo Ruiz Senior Center building on 50 Rizal Street where a six-story high mural entitled "Ang Lipi ni Lapu Lapu" (The Descendants of Lapu Lapu) immortalizes some important personalities in Philippine and U.S, history.

Lapu Lapu, the fierce datu (chieftain) of Mactan (an island off the coast of Cebu province), is revered as the first Filipino hero. His tribe and its unique combat technique and strategy overwhelmed the European conquistador, Ferdinand Magellan, and his men.

Resisting attempts to be colonized, Lapu Lapu and his warriors were believed to have attacked them with an aggressive barrage, combining kampilan (swordsmanship), arnis or kali (stick fighting), and suntukan (fist fighting) skills. Thus, even with their superior weapons and armor, Magellan and his men were soundly defeated. Magellan himself was killed. Humiliated by the loss to "uncivilized" indios (natives), it took Spain another 50 years before sending its next expedition to Asia.

Gazing up at the imposing mural, our students would try to identify other familiar faces. One thought he recognized one of them, a brown-skinned boxer. "Is that Manny Pacquiao?" Good guess, but it is actually Pancho Villa, the first Filipino boxer who made his mark in American sports history decades before Manny "Pacman" Pacquiao.

Pancho Villa (August 1, 1901 - July 14, 1925) was the first Filipino and Asian world champion in boxing. Genetically, from Pancho to Pacquiao, Filipino boxers must have inherited their distinct speed (*bilis*) and power (*lakas*) from the cunning Lapu Lapu.

The oversized portrait of Pancho Villa in the San Francisco mural is somewhat deceptive because he was really a small man, just 5'1" and weighed only 114 pounds. He is the smallest of the outstanding Filipino professional boxers featured in this book. Despite his physical size, Pancho Villa is certainly not small in terms of his ring accomplishments. This is probably why muralists Johanna Poethig, Vic Clemente, and Presco Tabios portrayed him like a giant at the top center of their mural.

Pancho Villa became the World flyweight champion in 1923. The Associated Press named him "Flyweight Fighter of the Century" in 1989. He was inducted into the International Boxing Hall of Fame in 1994 and voted one of *The Ring*'s "80 Best Fighters of the Last 80 years" in 2002. This last accolade carries high recognition and prestige since *The Ring* is one of the oldest and most respected boxing publications in the world. Hence, it is nicknamed "the bible of boxing." Pancho Villa and heavyweight champion Jack Dempsey were the first ones to be awarded *The Ring* world title belts.

Pancho Villa is the only boxer in this book who was never knocked out in more than 100 professional bouts. He also has the highest winning percentage – almost 90 percent – for 92 wins out of 104 total fights, and only eight losses and four draws. With this record, it is no wonder that Pancho Villa is considered one of the greatest boxers of all time.

Amazingly, this descendant of Lapu Lapu knocked out 24 opponents almost all of whom were much taller than him. Like Lapu Lapu, Pancho Villa was not deterred by his disadvantage in height. Instead, he used it to his advantage.

With a body mass that was closer to the ground, he had a lower center of gravity. This gave him the ability to shift weight and move faster in any direction without losing balance, while maintaining speed and power. From his lower vantage point, he delivered stiff probing inside straights and hooks to his opponent's body, and finished off with a penetrating right upper cut to the chin or digs to the hanging ribs. To counter him, taller opponents had to maneuver from the outside in an unconventional manner and are forced to bend down into an awkward, easily off-balanced stance.

Beginnings in the Philippines

Pancho Villa was born on August 1, 1901. Baptized Francisco Villaruel Guilledo, he grew up in the sleepy town of La Carlota in Negros Occidental. The Guilledo family lived and worked on the hacienda of Don Victoriano Rodriguez. His father, Rafael, and mother, Maria Villaruel, parted ways before Francisco turned a year old. Rafael decided to try his luck in Manila and eventually joined the U.S. Navy. Francisco then grew up with his mother, raising goats and occasionally helping cut sugarcane in the vast plantation.

When he was 11 years old, Francisco was convinced by his friend, Manuel, to go with him to the big and bustling city of Iloilo. There they found work as shoe shine boys and doing odd jobs. After a few years, Manuel and Francisco decided that they were not making enough money to send back to their families so they stowed away on an inter-island ship to Manila, the famous capital of the country. Everyone from the provinces thought Manila had "streets paved with gold." Arriving in Manila was intimidating for the two stowaways. They ended up sleeping on the floor of the old Olympic Stadium before they found a room to rent in the Santa Cruz neighborhood.

The child who would become Pancho Villa had aspirations of getting a better job or joining the U.S. Navy, and that led him to go back to school. While attending elementary school classes, he met Elino Flores who took him to the gym where he and his brothers practiced boxing. After watching a few practice sessions and hearing the rags-to-riches stories straight from the mouths of prizefighters, Francisco was convinced that he should also earn money in the ring.

He stopped going to school and instead trained long and hard, quickly learning the fundamentals by watching the older boxers. At a gym in Tondo, Manila, he became the regular sparring partner of Elino. During a sparring session, the 5'1" Francisco's speed and powerful delivery caught the 5'6" Elino on the chin and floored him. Observing at a corner visibly impressed was the business executive Paquito Villa, a boxing promoter.

Attracted by Francisco's potential, Paquito invited him to be part of his stable of boxers, which included Dencio Cabanela, Apolonio Gener, Johnny Hill, and the Flores brothers. Over the years, Paquito treated the 17-year old like a son and eventually adopted him, changing his name to Pancho Villa, after the Mexican revolutionary. During his years of training in Tondo, the boxer now known as Pancho would develop strong legs and solid physique.

Pancho Villa displaying his *suntukan* stance
Photo credit: Tony Triem

Pancho Villa's first professional bout in Manila was against Kid Castro in 1919. He fought close to 50 bouts, many at the famous Olympic Club. Not only did he defeat local Filipino sluggers like Valentin Santos, Pete Sarmiento, Max Mason, Leoncio Bernabe, and Battling Ongay, Pancho Villa also won against visiting Australians Syd Keenan and Jimmy Taylor; Sacramento, California native Georgie Lee and Seattle, Washington-based Eddie Moore.

Pancho prevailed six times against the taller, heavier and more experienced Mike "Young" Ballerino from New Jersey. Only two years after turning pro, he defeated some big-name boxers including Terio Pandong for the Philippine flyweight title. He also knocked out George Mendies, the reigning Australian flyweight and bantamweight champion.

With his string of impressive victories, it did not take long before Frank E. Churchill, an American boxing promoter, took Pancho Villa under his wings. Churchill, in partnership with Joe Waterman and the brothers Eddie and Stewart Tait, shuttled back and forth between the U.S. and the Philippines, managing and promoting. They were filling boxing cards not just in Manila but also in U.S. cities eager to host exciting and new talents from all over the world. Churchill brought many Filipino prizefighters to the U.S. including Speedy Dado, Clever Sencio, Dencio Cabanela, and Elino Flores. Frank Churchill and Paquito Villa became Pancho's managers.

Remarkable Record

In just six years as a professional boxer, Pancho Villa fought 104 bouts, an average of 17 fights a year. He was in the ring practically every month!

His boxing career almost ended in early 1922, however, when he decided to return to his hometown in Negros Occidental to retire. This was because the father of his girlfriend, Gliceria Concepcion, disapproved of him since he was "a mere boxer."

Filipino boxing fans protested Pancho Villa's sudden decision and clamored for him to reconsider. What convinced him to step back into the ring was a telegram invitation from the legendary sports promoter George Lewis "Tex" Rickard to fight in the United States. It was a difficult invitation to refuse since Rickard was the Bob Arum of that era.

Pancho's managers, Churchill and Paquito Villa, convinced him of the lucrative opportunities for him in the United States. He would have a shot at a world title and he would be paid well. Thus, on May 1922, he boarded the SS President Grant for New York with his two managers, and his good friend and fellow boxer, Elino Flores. His U.S.-based *kababayans* (countrymen) from the East Coast to the West Coast welcomed his presence and became his ardent supporters.

From June 1922 to April 1925, Pancho Villa fought the other half of his colorful boxing career in the U.S. and Canada.

His American boxing journey started slow—two stirring newspaper decision (NWS) defeats versus hometown favorites, Abe Goldstein and Frankie Genaro, in New Jersey. Challenged to do better, he put up a string of confidence building wins which led to the American flyweight championship against Johnny Buff before a sell-out crowd at Ebbet's Field, Brooklyn, New York.

Pancho Villa knocked down the defending champion twice, winning the title in an upset. He now had the full attention of the American boxing community and even landed in the January 1923 cover of *The Ring* magazine. On a roll, in June 1923, he knocked out Jimmy "The Mighty Atom" Wilde with a hammer right to the jaw in the 7th round, thus grabbing his World flyweight title and going down in history as the first Filipino world boxing champion.

In Pancho Villa's only bout in Canada, the *Toronto Star* detailed how he defeated local boy, Donnie Mack,

> *When the fourth round came up, Villa winked at his manager, Frank Churchill, darted across the ring, leaped at the Toronto kid and left-hooked him to the floor for "eight." Mack got up and tried to fight his way into a clinch, but the little Filipino roused to his job, shook him off, and after these exchanges, slammed over a series of lightning-like lefts and rights and Mack counted the daises...It was half a minute before the Toronto lad recovered his scattered senses.*

While based in the U.S., Pancho Villa fought the likes of Terry Martin, Abe Friedman, Benny Schwartz, George

Marks, Danny Edwards, Frankie Ash, Bud Taylor, among many other boxing greats. He was so popular among promoters that he was receiving US$20,000 per fight. His gross earnings totaled US$250,000, which catapulted him from rags to riches in a very short time.

With the money he had, Pancho Villa spent like the sports icon he was at that time, especially in the company of celebrities like heavyweight champion Jack Dempsey. They bet on horses together at the racetrack. He rode a flashy US$10,000 Lincoln custom-built car. Walking down 5th Avenue with his entourage, Pancho Villa bought designer suits and generously tipped waiters and musicians at New York's fanciest restaurants. The sports celebrity was also known to buy expensive gifts for the women he fancied, including a Miss New York pageant winner.

An American sports scribe wrote this comment on Pancho Villa's celebrity lifestyle:

> As World Champion, Villa collected into his person all the swank and swagger of the period, and the whole country felt an electrifying pride in his rise from rags to riches, his magnificent wardrobe, his collection of silk shirts, and natty hats, his pearl buttons and gold cufflinks, and his royal retinue. He had a servant to massage him, another to towel him, a valet to put on his shoes, another to help him put on his trousers, still another valet to comb his hair, to powder his cheeks, and spray him

> *with the most expensive perfume. (Quoted from Dennis Villegas, May 9, 2006, "Pancho Villa: First Filipino World Boxing Champion" pilipinokomiks.blogspot.com)*

Audiences from Oakland, California to Boston, Massachusetts who watched Pancho Villa's fights remembered him not only for his tenacity and ring generalship but also for his clean and respectful ways in the ring. Whenever his opponent was down, he would step away quickly without waiting for the referee to tell him to do so. If his opponent did not get up, Pancho Villa would always show sincere concern. Lapu Lapu's descendant did this gracious act in a boxing era that, at times, was cutthroat and characterized by "winning by all means possible." In their quest to win, some pugilists would hit adversaries who were still down or on their knees.

Pancho Villa came home in September 1924 to a hero's welcome in Manila and his home province of Negros Occidental. He would fight his last Philippine bouts during his homecoming visit, defeating Clever Sencio in Wallace Field and Francisco Pilapil in Iloilo City.

In a tragic turn of events, after losing a non-title fight with Jimmy McLarnin in Oakland, California, Pancho Villa would succumb to complications associated with a tooth infection that had spread to his throat. He was just 23 years old and at the peak of his career. His widow, Gliceria Concepcion, who he was able to marry against the will of her father, believed that Pancho Villa was deliberately poisoned by a gambling syndicate. He was a great loss to the Philippines, the U.S. and the entire boxing world.

2

Bolo Punch

"Kung di ukol, di bubukol."
(What isn't meant to be will not happen.)

On the six-story mural in San Francisco's San Lorenzo Ruiz Senior Center, Pancho Villa's portrait is surrounded by those of other descendants of Lapu Lapu who ventured to the United States.

The earliest Filipino settlers in America were seamen who jumped ship from the Manila-Acapulco galleons and settled either in Acapulco, Mexico or the bayous of Louisiana where they built a Manila fishing village.

The Filipino migrants who cheered on Pancho Villa in the 1920s had left their families in the Philippines for greener pastures in the U.S. Most of them were contracted by American labor recruiters as agricultural workers in the sprawling fields, farms, orchards, vineyards and plantations of Hawaii, California, Oregon, and Washington. Some went as far north as Alaska to work in the fish, shrimp, and crab industries, including the seafood canneries.

Others worked in the hotels, restaurants, residences, hospitals, trains, and service jobs in big cities like New York, Chicago, San Francisco, and Los Angeles, as cooks, waiters, doormen, valets, conductors, butlers, mechanics, maintenance workers, gardeners, dishwashers, painters, carpenters, plumbers, drivers, dockhands, etc. It was also common for poor rural boys to join the U.S. Army but they had to have finished some formal schooling.

Those who were not qualified but had boxing talent were enticed by American promoters to fight professionally in the U.S., a group that included Pancho Villa and another pugilist named Ceferino Garcia (August 26, 1906 - January 1, 1981).

With the sudden death of Pancho Villa in July 1925, the large Filipino migrant community lost a *kuya* (elder brother) they all looked up to and admired. Not only was Villa a very exciting boxer to watch, read about or listen to, he was also the quintessential Filipino success story who made them feel that it was possible to for them to reach the American dream and be equal or even better than a white man.

The Filipino migrant community needed another dominating *kababayan* (compatriot) slugger who would lift their spirits and pride. The rise of Ceferino Garcia, a Visayan boxer like Pancho Villa, in the 1930s was their answer. Garcia was known to American boxing aficionados as the inventor of the lethal "bolo punch." It is called such because the execution is similar to the crouched swift sweeping semi-hook, semi-uppercut motion necessary to cut *tubo* (sugarcane) with a bolo knife (similar to a machete).

The bolo punch motion is intuitive to many descendants of Lapu Lapu. For centuries, poor *indio* plantation workers harvested sugarcane at the sprawling mestizo-owned haciendas found all over the archipelago, especially in the Visayan provinces of Negros and Leyte where Pancho Villa and Ceferino Garcia came from.

The bolo was both a farming tool and a protective weapon so it was common for men to be proficient with its striking technique. Garcia and his compatriots took advantage of the bolo punch's deceptive and swift delivery to knockout opponents, which made for interesting news write-ups.

Another Filipino pugilist, Macario Flores, one of the Tondo-trained Flores boxing brothers, was also known to have popularized the bolo punch with Garcia in the U.S. in the 1920s and 1930s. Elino, Macario's brother, was Pancho Villa's sparring partner.

Famous bolo punchers include champions from around the globe, from different weight divisions and from different decades: Americans Sugar Ray Leonard (welterweight, middleweight) and Roy Jones Jr. (middleweight, heavyweight) Britain's Joe Calzaghe (super middleweight, light heavyweight), Cuba's Kid Gavilan (welterweight), Nigeria's Ike Ibeabuchi (heavyweight), among many others.

Variations of the bolo punch are used in Chinese, Japanese, Thai, Burmese, European, and Latino-style boxing and even other martial arts and combative sports.

Armed with a big heart and his secret weapon, Garcia bolo punched his way to 142 bouts in a career spanning 22 years. He is the only true Filipino world middleweight champion (1939-1940). His 102 career victories and astonishing 67 KOs, are the most for any Filipino prizefighter, past and present. Not even boxing legends Flash Elorde, Pancho Villa or Manny Pacquiao could surpass his wins and KO feats.

Garcia would also win coveted welterweight boxing titles in the Philippines and California. He was inducted into *The Ring*'s Boxing Hall of Fame in 1977, the World Boxing Hall of Fame in 1989, and the Philippine Sports Commission (PSC) Hall of Fame in 2010 (along with Pancho Villa and Flash Elorde). However, Garcia is long overdue for recognition as part of the crème de la crème in the New York-based International Boxing Hall of Fame (IBHF).

Besides boxing, Mr. Bolo Punch's other claim to fame is as the driver and bodyguard for actress Mae West. She enjoyed talking to Garcia about boxing since her father, Battlin Jack West, was also a prizefighter.

Garcia also worked as an extra in a few Hollywood movies, such as "Hollywood Canteen" in 1944, "Joe Palooka Champ" in 1946, "Body and Soul" in 1947, and "Whiplash" in 1948. He also had a cameo role in the John Wayne film "Back to Bataan" in 1945.

In World War II, he even joined Shirley Temple in a radio broadcast encouraging allied soldiers to continue the fight until victory. Popular among Filipinos not just in the fields but also in the army during those times, Garcia was an inspiration to his *kababayans* in the First and Second Filipino Infantry Regiments. U.S. President Dwight Eisenhower singled him out publicly in a White House press statement for this commitment which inspired and lifted the spirits of the troops in the U.S. and the Philippines.

Beginnings in the Philippines

Raised in the town of Naval in Biliran Province (formerly a part of Leyte Province), Ceferino Garcia was the eldest of six children of Fortunato Garcia and Pascuala Pieras. He was baptized Cipriano and was known as "Predo" to his family in Biliran. His name was "Americanized" to Ceferino when he came to the U.S. His siblings remember him as a hyperactive child who could never concentrate on his school work. They were not surprised when he decided to drop out of school in the first grade, distracted by petty gambling, particularly heads-or-tails and pool table betting.

Quarrels would often erupt. During those days, disputes among kids were settled with a combination of *suntukan* (fist fighting), *dumogan* (grappling/wrestling), *sikohan* (elbowing), and *tadyakan* (kicking). *Suntukan* was Garcia's forte. By age 15, he had become a dreaded street fighter who had earned a reputation all over town as a person "never to contend with."

Garcia was built physically strong and quite skillful with his hands which allowed him to work as a blacksmith and later on as a baker. His younger brother, Alberto, idolized him for his ability to craft sharp bolo knives with strong, well-timed blows from a heavy sledge hammer.

When he was 15, Garcia left the sleepy town of Naval for faster-paced Cebu City to look for better work opportunities. While working at a bakery, Garcia met former boxer and promoter, Jesus Cortez, who brought him to Manila where he was introduced to American promoter Frank Churchill. Thus began his boxing career.

Garcia's debut bouts in Manila in mid-1923 started out slow—three draws, once with Pedro del Mundo and twice with Irineo Flores. By the time his career picked up in 1926, Pancho Villa had become but a sad memory in the minds of the Filipino public. Meanwhile, the Manila boxing headlines were filled with descriptions of thrilling flyweight fights featuring Little Pancho (Villa's younger half-brother), the Flores brothers, Kid Dencio, Pablo Dano, Speedy Dado, among others.

Between 1926 and 1931, promoter Churchill would match Garcia against local and visiting American welterweight prizefighters such as Harry Stone, Ignacio Fernandez, Joe Hall, Joe Sacramento, Frank Malinao, and Tony Gora.

In 1928, Garcia outpointed Spanish-Filipino mestizo Luis Logan in 12 rounds at the Olympic Stadium to gain his first boxing title—welterweight champion of the Orient. After successfully defending his title four times in 1931, Churchill decided he was ready to be battle tested among the best in the U.S.

Fighting in America

Compared to his not-so-exciting ring performances in the Philippines, almost all of which ended in judges' decisions or draws and just one KO, Garcia had a colorful 13-year (1932-1945) career in the U.S.

Following Frank Churchill's death in March 1933, Garcia was mentored by another highly regarded American manager, George Parnassus, out of Los Angeles, California. His trainer was a Filipino named Johnny Villaflores.

Under his new promoter and trainer, Garcia faced many world-class contenders including Henry Armstrong, Fred Apostoli, Anton Christoforidis, Young Corbett III, Lloyd Marshall, Ken Overlin, Barney Ross, Billy Soose, and Freddie Steele. The Filipino pugilist did not disappoint his managers, Churchill and Parnassus. The transplant from Biliran won the annual competition for the California State welterweight title in 1932, 1933, 1934, and 1935.

Henry Armstrong and Garcia at their pre-fight medical exam
Photo credit: Tracy Callis

On September 23, 1937, Garcia first had a shot for a world title in the welterweight division. However, Barney Ross bested him by unanimous decision. A year later, Parnassus decided to place his bolo punching ward in cards for a higher weight division. His gamble paid off.

In October 1939, Garcia floored Californian Fred Apostoli three times in Madison Square Garden to win the world middleweight championship. In 1939, his world middleweight title defense against Nebraska-native Glen Lee was held at Manila's Rizal Football Stadium in front of 40,000 cheering fans and was refereed by the legendary Jack Dempsey. The bout was the first world title fight to be held in the Philippines.

Garcia successfully defended that title against Glen Lee, Henry Armstrong, and Allen Matthews but lost it to Virginian Ken Overlin in May 1940 by unanimous decision. California State University professor Linda España-Maram quotes the *New York Times'* admiration of the Filipino pugilist:

Garcia embodies everything that goes to make a titleholder…He is strong. He can box. He can punch. He can absorb punishment. He can adjust himself to ring situations as they develop, is resourceful, alert, cool under fire, a perfect fury when the tide swings his way.

In his more-than-a-decade stint in the U.S., Garcia conquered seasoned hometown favorites not just from America but all over the world, such as Lloyd Marshall, Bobby Pacho, Walter "Popeye" Woods, Al Trulmans, Jackie Burke, Dick Foster, Peter Jackson, Cleto Locatelli, Leon Zorrita, George Salvadore, Al Manfredo, Joe Gans, Sammy O'Dell, Sammy Brown, Bep van Klaveren, Andy DiVodi, Sal Sorio, Joe Glick, Jimmy Evans, King Tut, Meyer Grace, Johnny "Bandit" Romero, Jimmy Duffy, and Tommy King.

In Los Angeles, Garcia outpointed Dutch Olympic gold medalist-turned-professional boxer Bep van Klaveren in 1934. A decade later, in October 1944, he surprised Tepito legend Luis "Kid Azteca" Villanueva (101 wins), before the Mexican's widely cheering fans in Mexico City. This was the second time he beat Kid Azteca. Garcia was actually the first Filipino "Mexicutioner," not Manny Pacquiao.

Unlike in the Philippines where Garcia was able to deliver just one KO defeat, he knocked out opponents in more than half of his total fights—a total of 67 KOs, many of them via his trademark bolo punch—in the U.S.

In June 1932, in a packed Oakland Auditorium, he went against homeboy Jimmy "Oakland" Duffy. The local

GARCIA WHIPS GLEN LEE AT GILMORE STADIUM

Filipino Scores Surprising Upset to Give Nebraska Wildcat Sound Drubbing

Ceferino Garcia spotted Glen Lee nearly ten pounds in weight and a 10-8 bulge in the betting odds but came through with a decisive ten-round victory over the Nebraskan in the Hollywood Legion's summer opener at Gilmore Stadium last night.

May 7th, 1938 *Los Angeles Times* article
Photo credit: Tracy Callis

favorite was leading in points until Garcia landed a smashing bolo punch which broke Duffy's jaw and sent him to the canvas in the seventh. Later, in Santa Monica, California, Garcia, again behind on points, turned the tables on Willis Johnson when he connected with his dreaded bolo punch, flooring Johnson five times before the bout was stopped.

Whenever Garcia fought in Stockton, Watsonville, and Sacramento, the venues would be jammed with his *kababayans*, who would take time off from their backbreaking farm jobs, dress up in their best suits, and wait for him to unleash his famous bolo punch. In Stockton on July 3, 1934, they roared loudly when he floored the veteran Andy DiVodi in the first round with just two solid punches.

Garcia retired in 1945 and settled down with his family in Southern California. He passed away in San Diego in 1981 and is buried in North Hollywood, California. He had three children: daughters Maureen and Vicki and son Ceferino Jr.

Mr. Bolo Punch will always be remembered as the descendant of Lapu Lapu who became world middleweight champion and had the highest number of wins (102!) in Philippine boxing history. This record will probably never be surpassed.

In August 2011, *The Ring* named Ceferino Garcia the third "Greatest Filipino Fighter of All-Time." Well, International Boxing Hall of Fame, 90 million Filipinos and the rest of the boxing world are patiently waiting for your recognition. It is time.

3

Magnificent Four

Filipinos and Filipino immigrants in the United States found their idols in these pugilists. Boxing enthusiasts celebrated victories, challenged unpopular decisions, and lamented losses in both countries. Commuting between the United States and the Philippines, fighters became a force that bridged the Filipino and Filipino American experiences.

-Professor Linda España-Maram

Our students on the Filipino ethno-tour of San Francisco also stopped at a 90-foot Corinthian column in the middle of the ritzy Union Square shopping district. Engraved on the stone is the story of the U.S. annexation of the Philippines in 1898. It details how the U.S. Navy's Pacific Fleet destroyed the once powerful Spanish armada. The golden goddess of victory on top of the column symbolizes the beginning of the American empire. We tell them that the colonization of the Philippines brought American capitalist economics, American political institutions, and American sports and recreations like baseball, basketball, and of course, boxing.

The introduction of American-style boxing in the Philippines influenced the early combative art of *suntukan* (or *panuntukan*) practiced by Lapu Lapu and his descendants. Conversely, Filipino sluggers introduced unique body movements and techniques [to American boxing] such as their *galaw ng paa* (footwork), *kilos* (movement), *liko* (turns), *ikot* (pivot), *lihis* (deviate), to their *ilag* (ducking and weaving). They also exhibited distinct boxing traits like their *bilis* (speed), *liksi* (agility), *talino* (cleverness), *lakas* (power), *ilap* (elusiveness), and *tibay* (sturdiness). Filipino boxers merged these techniques and traits into American-style boxing especially at the bantamweight, flyweight, featherweight, and lightweight classes.

U.S. Army and Navy soldier/boxers were the first to expose the local Filipino boys to American-style boxing. The U.S. annexation of the Philippines brought white and black American pugilists who served in the military in Manila, like lightweight Mike "Young" Ballerino and African American heavyweights Demon White and Joe Blackburn.

Not long after, Filipinos who joined the U.S. Navy, such as Eddie Duarte and Manuel Soriano, emerged as contenders. The YMCA of Manila and the many young men's clubs that mushroomed all over the archipelago started offering boxing as part of their fitness and recreational activities. Boxing supposedly helped keep young men away from the evils of drugs, gambling, prostitution, and alcohol, according to Joseph Svinth in his *Journal of Combative Sport*'s article "The Origins of Philippines Boxing, 1899-1929."

For those who wanted to get to the professional level, there was the Olympic Club in Manila, established in 1909. A converted cock fighting arena, this was the epicenter of boxing—amateur and professional—during this period. Additionally, the Olympic was a sports stadium and the recruitment office of American entertainment recruiter/manager/promoter and agent Frank Churchill and the Tait brothers (Stewart and Eddie). African American lightweight champion Rufus "Rufe" Turner helped train boxers while Joe Waterman was assigned to scout for talents in the remote towns and barrios. Everyone knew that anyone wanting to make it big in boxing needed to catch the attention of these gentlemen. Waterman filled bout cards from Seattle, to Portland, all the way down to Los Angeles.

In the 1920s and 1930s, the Olympic, the Manila Stadium (renamed Rizal Memorial Stadium), and many other venues all over the islands would be packed to the rafters during fight nights. Boxing's popularity peaked when prizefighting was legalized in 1921. Featured local favorites were the Flores brothers, Macario, Francisco, Elino and Irineo; Dencio Cabanela, Sylvino Jamito, Apolonio Gener, Lope Tenorio, Varias Milling, Pete Sarmiento, Gene Espinosa, among others. Scouts and promoters brought in talents from everywhere and they did not fail to please the crowds, both domestically and internationally.

From Bato, Leyte, Pablo Dano (153 fights: 83 wins, 45 losses, 24 draws, with 29 KOs), did only one professional fight in Manila versus Varias Milling on September 1926, before leaving for Singapore and the U.S. Dano would become the 1929 flyweight champion of the Orient.

One bantamweight boxer, Joe Mendiola alias Kid Natcho, was in 158 fights, probably the most among any Filipino prizefighter, and had an impressive 74 wins, 48 losses, 34 draws, with 27 KOs, but he never won any boxing title. Unlike most of his peers who would go to the U.S. after bouts in the Philippines, Mendiola fought all over Western Europe for five years (1930-1935). The 5'1" Kid Natcho was the most successful Filipino there with 43 wins accumulated from bouts in France, Switzerland, Belgium, the United Kingdom, Spain, and Italy.

Pancho Villa inspired many of these boxers who had similar rags-to-riches stories which brought them from their provincial hometowns, then to Manila, and finally to duel in international venues. At stake were world- and American boxing titles and of course, thousands of dollars in purses. Everyone wanted to be the next Pancho Villa. Many were called but few were chosen.

In this chapter, we discuss the "Magnificent Four" who tried their best to fit into Pancho Villa's giant gloves: Little Pancho (January 9, 1912 - May 5, 1969), Small Montana (February 24, 1913 - August 4, 1976), Little Dado (January 1, 1916 - July 7, 1965), and Speedy Dado (December 25, 1906 - July 2, 1990).

These four Philippine-bred prizefighters stood out among the many who fought in America during the '30s and early '40s, decades after the demise of Pancho Villa. They filled the void in the hearts of the growing Filipino migrant population, especially in the West Coast and all the way to Hawaii. They entertained and amazed the American audiences and sports writers with their ring tenacity and determination, in addition to their *suntukan*-inspired moves.

None of the Magnificent Four stood more than 5"4" in height and each weighed no more than 118 pounds, and yet they were the formidable Filipino foes of aspiring American and European flyweight and bantamweight world titlists of their era. Then, there were no multiple world title sanctioning bodies (i.e. WBA, WBO, WBC, IBF, IBO, *The Ring*, etc.)— just the powerful New York State Athletic Commission and the not-as-influential California State Athletic Commission. Additionally, the Philippine Games and Amusement Board (GAB) and its national title belts only came into existence in 1951. By that time, these four gentlemen had retired.

Eulogio "Little Pancho" Tingson (44-14-15, 8 KO)

The first of the Magnificent Four who followed Pancho Villa's journey into the ring was Eulogio Tingson, his younger half-brother. Villa's estranged father, Rafael Guilledo met Tingson's mother while he was in Manila prior to joining the U.S. Navy. Thus, unlike Villa who was raised in Negros Occidental, Tingson was brought up in Manila.

He was only 13 years old when his older brother died in 1925. Inspired by the legacy of his sibling, Tingson turned professional at the early age of 16. Managed by Jerry Zukor, he aptly chose the moniker "Little Pancho" even though at 5'3", he was two inches taller than his *kuya* (elder brother).

He boxed in Manila for two years, from 1928-30. His career started quite slow: two wins, three losses, and three

Little Pancho shows of a picture of his older brother, Pancho Villa
Photo credit: Tony Triem

draws. It did not skyrocket like his brother's. Disappointed, Little Pancho took a year off to refine his technique and to try to get an agent to bring him to the U.S.

An opportunity opened in March 1932 at the Honolulu Auditorium. He was pitted against the more experienced flyweight Midget Wolgast twice. Many of the spectators thought that he was winning against the Philadelphia veteran. But Little Pancho lost a very controversial decision and ended up with another controversial draw in the rematch bout. Both contests were witnessed by many migrant Filipino farm workers who booed the results in protest. Thousands called for a boycott of Filipino boxing in Hawaii.

Little Pancho performed at 30 fights all over the U.S. from March 1932 to September 1934. After the slow start in Hawaii, he would win 19 bouts, with KOs over Oklahoman Dude McCook (4th round) and Californian Al Romero (8th round).

The highlight of his two years in the U.S. came in February 1934 when Little Pancho knocked out his older brother's nemesis, Frankie Genaro, with a speedy two-punch combination in the eighth round at the Oakland Auditorium in California. His two-year U.S. contract ended in October 1934, so from December 1934 to November 1937, he was back in the Philippines.

While at home, Little Pancho racked up an impressive 12 victories and zero losses, including beating the formidable Little Dado four times and drawing him once. He captured the Oriental bantamweight title by defeating Joe Mendiola three times in Manila. In March 1938, he returned to Honolulu to begin a second U.S. boxing assignment. On his third fight, Little Pancho knocked out "The Rose of San Jose" Jackie Jurich in the 10th round to win the American bantamweight crown. He would also knockdown and beat compatriot Small Montana at the Oakland Auditorium in January 1940.

Benjamin "Small Montana" Gan (83-25-10, 13 KO)

The second member of the Magnificent Four is a bright-eyed southpaw who was popularly known as Small Montana. At 5'4", he was the "tallest" among the four. Small Montana was a Filipino and Chinese mestizo, born Benjamin Gan. Like Pancho Villa, he was raised in La Carlota, Negros Occidental where his father was chief of police. Small Montana grew up dreaming to be a Pancho Villa someday. He was so inspired by his legendary provincemate that he kept a picture of him in his wallet. In 1930, he left home and sailed for Manila to become a prizefighter.

By 1931, the 18-year old had won his first professional bout against Little Ligaspe. He was undefeated for two years and would win 25 straight bouts in Manila, Hawaii, and California before losing to Kid Oriolo in January 1933. Small Montana earned a reputation for his quick punches and for being a small but scrappy and smart fighter. He won the World flyweight title (New York version) twice with decisions over Midget Wolgast and Tuffy Pierpont in 1935. He lost the title to the legendary Benny Lynch at a 1937 match in London.

During his decade-long ring career, Small Montana prevailed over the likes of Manuel Ortiz, Midget Wolgast, Tony Marino, Joe Tei Ken, Speedy Dado, Tommy Forte, Augie Curtis, Pat Palmer, Frankie Jarr, Eugene "Tuffy" Pierpont, and Antol "Tony" Kocsis. The Negros-native fought fellow Filipino

Small Montana and Little Dado with their
fight promoter and managers
Photo credit: Tony Triem

flyweights Little Dado and Little Pancho but lost to both of them on points. In August 2011, *The Ring*, named him seventh "Greatest Filipino Fighter of All-Time."

Eleuterio "Little Dado" Zapanta (46-7-9, 21 KO)

The third member of our Magnificent Four is Eleuterio Zapanta, alias "Little Dado." Despite his size – 5'2" in height and weighing around 115 pounds -- there was nothing "little" about his ring accomplishments.

After a slow start and learning from four straight losses to Little Pancho, Little Dado recouped and never lost again in 51 straight fights. Now that's a feat! What makes this record unimaginable these days is that he was virtually in the ring every three weeks for three years straight (April 1937 to February 1941). Little Dado would electrify the crowd with 11 KOs and 9 TKOs. That is why *The Ring* rated him among the top five flyweights in the world for five consecutive years.

In those 51 fights, the tiny boxer from Negros Occidental would take home the California State bantamweight title four times (1938-1939), the World bantamweight title (1940), the World flyweight title (1941), and the National Boxing Association flyweight title (1941). He would prevail over tried and tested bantamweights and flyweights like Yoichiro Hanada, Young Joe Roche, Tommy Cobb, Jimmy "Babe" McCusker, Henry Hook, and Tony Olivera. No wonder Little Dado was one of the most remembered darlings of the Little Manila communities in Watsonville, Stockton, and Los Angeles during the 1930s and 1940s.

From 1938-1943, Little Dado was ranked in the top five in the Flyweight division by *The Ring* magazine—attaining the #1 overall rating in 1939. For this feat, he is consistently rated as one of the greatest Filipino boxers in history by many sports writers, bloggers, and publications. In 1943, Little Dado aspired to win the world featherweight title, hoping to become the second slugger to ever hold three different world titles simultaneously. He failed and retired. But, in August 2011, *The Ring*, recognized him as the sixth "Greatest Filipino Fighter of All-Time."

Diosdado "Speedy Dado" Posadas (90-43-14, 37 KO)

The last member of our Magnificent Four is Manila-born Diosdado "Speedy Dado" Posadas, named so because of his many outstanding feats. His other alias is "Brown Doll" due to his smooth brown complexion and baby-doll face. He is the only true bantamweight among his contemporaries in the 1930s highlighted in this chapter.

In a career that spanned a decade and a half, he would fight 147 times. This is more than the fight totals of Pancho Villa, Ceferino Garcia, Little Pancho, Small Montana, and Little Dado, combined. Like Mr. Bolo Punch, Speedy Dado was also managed by Jesus Cortez and Frank Churchill. The latter thought that he would actually become the next Pancho Villa.

Speedy Dado fought more than twice the number of fights than Little Pancho and had the same high 60 percent winning margin. Remarkably, Speedy Dado would not lose in 26 consecutive bouts from 1926-1928, an average of one win per month for those two years in both the Philippines and U.S.

Speedy Dado shares a light moment with Gene Espinosa
Photo credit: Tracy Callis

He never lost a bout in the Philippines. Most importantly, Speedy Dado would win the California bantamweight title four times (versus Newsboy Brown once, Joe Tei Ken once, and Young Tommy twice). However, he only held the California title for short periods of time and disappointingly, he never won the battles during world title matches.

Nevertheless, Speedy Dado defeated Lou Salica and Panama Al Brown, and drew with Midget Wolgast, all of whom held championships during their career. He retired in Los Angeles, and like middleweight Ceferino Garcia, was employed by Hollywood actress Mae West as a chauffeur. *The Ring* recognized Speedy Dado with an honorable mention in their article on the "Greatest Filipino Fighters of All-Time."

4

Flash

"Ang bayaning nasusugatan, nagiibayo ang tapang."
(A patriot who is wounded becomes more courageous.)

The end of World War II and the granting of Philippine independence by the United States on July 4, 1946 would usher in three events which significantly affected Filipino professional boxing in the 1950s through the 1960s.

First was the emergence of promoter and manager Lope "Papa" Sarreal. The equivalent of kingmakers Don King or Bob Arum in the Asia Pacific region, Sarreal replaced Frank Churchill as Philippine boxing's main matchmaker. The entrepreneurial Sarreal would single-handedly expand international promotions beyond the U.S. and help intensify regional competitions within the Asia-Pacific.

An ambitious visionary, he would eventually organize more than 70 world title bouts and increase the development of big-time professional fighting in Japan, Thailand, China, Indonesia, Korea, and other Asian markets. As a manager,

Sarreal guided the career of 22 world champions, including flyweight Yoshio Shirai of Japan and welterweight Saensak Muangsurin of Thailand. For his significant impact on international boxing, Sarreal was named to the International Boxing Hall of Fame in 2005.

The second event was the genuine internationalization of boxing with the founding of three important regional and world-title granting and regulating organizations. In 1954, the Orient and Pacific Boxing Federation (OPBF) was formalized and named its first official roster of OPBF titleholders which included: Danny Kid (Philippines), flyweight; Keeichi Momoro (Japan), bantamweight; Shigeji Kaneko (Japan), featherweight; Leo Alonzo (Philippines), lightweight; and Hachiro Tasumi (Japan), middleweight.

This bold move by Asian boxing leaders prodded U.S and Latin American principals to step-up their game. So in 1962, the National Boxing Association (NBA) was reorganized and renamed the World Boxing Association (WBA). Then on Valentine's Day in 1963, the Philippines along with 10 other countries established the World Boxing Council (WBC) in Mexico City. Prior to the creation of the OPBF, WBA, and WBC, regional and world titles as well as regulations and promotions were monopolized by U.S. promoters and state commissions. From then on, Filipinos and other non-American boxers did not have to fight primarily in the U.S., to be judged and refereed by Americans, to win a world title.

The third development was the long awaited rise

of another champion that descended from Lapu Lapu. The ascent of Gabriel "Flash" Elorde (March 25, 1935 – January 2, 1985) to the realm of champions in the 1960s would end a long title drought for a country thirsty for boxing heroes. A son-in-law of Papa Sarreal, Flash would become the first Filipino and Asian international boxing hall of famer.

The making of a world champion

In 1974, Elorde was recognized by the WBC as "the greatest world junior lightweight boxing champion in history". Every year from 1952 to 1967, he was involved in a national, regional, or world title bout. Thus, it came as no surprise when Elorde became the first Asian inducted into the World Boxing Hall of Fame in 1988 and the International Boxing Hall of Fame in 1993, even ahead of the legendary Pancho Villa.

In 2002, *The Ring* listed Elorde as one of "The 80 Greatest Boxers in the Past 80 years". He joined Pancho Villa as the only other Filipino on the list, which was topped by Sugar Ray Robinson, Henry Armstrong, Muhammad Ali, Joe Louis, among others. Forty years after he retired, many of Elorde's feats remain unsurpassed so he continues to be on many boxing aficionado's top 10 Filipino sluggers of all time.

His sustained stellar accomplishments became the gold standard for the other Filipino world champions of the '60s and '70s. Many would get world titles but could not approximate the high bar that Elorde set, including WBC champs Pedro Adigue, Jr. and Rene Barrientos, WBA champ

Bernabe Villacampo, and even WBA and WBC champ Erbito Salavarria.

Just like the other boxers in this book, Elorde came from very humble beginnings. He was born to a household of tenant farmers in Bogo, a small town not too far away from the big city of Cebu. At age 11, he left his family to try his luck in the bustling metropolis to the south. Like Pancho Villa, he started out as a shoe shine boy before finding work as a pin boy in a bowling alley.

As mentioned in the Garcia biography, Filipino kids then were fond of settling their disputes with *suntukan* (fist fighting). Elorde would realize his ring potential when he bloodied the face of an older and bigger bully. Encouraged by the result, he followed in the footsteps of his ring idols—Kid Independence and Tanny Campo and turned professional at 16 years old. The boy from Bogo would fight professionally for two decades, from 1951-1971.

Elorde began his career with 11 bouts in Cebu and would win 10 of them, knocking out eight opponents in the early rounds. Amazingly, these bouts happened only within six months—averaging two fights per month. The following year he won the vacant Orient and Pacific Boxing Federation bantamweight title against Hiroshi Horiguchi in Tokyo, Japan. The 17-year old Elorde caught the attention of the world, won the hearts of his countrymen and gained the respect of the Japanese aficionados. But that was just the beginning of a long reign.

Flash Elorde—one of the most charismatic
Filipino world champions

Photo credit: Tony Triem

The 5'5½" Elorde would compete in 44 title fights and 15 world title bouts with a record of 88 wins (33 KO), 27 losses and 2 draws. This was an exemplary feat for a super featherweight—a weight division that was crowded with contenders from the Philippines, the U.S. and elsewhere at that time. Despite the odds, he prevailed and garnered the OPBF Lightweight Championship, the Philippine Games and Amusement Board (GAB) Lightweight Championship, the Philippine GAB Super Featherweight Championship, the OPBF Bantamweight Championship, and the Philippine GAB Bantamweight Championship.

Normally, *suntukan* unfolds from a sequence of *sindak* (threats) and *duro* (taunts). Flash was a deft practitioner of both. Antagonizing his adversary created openings for him to come in with his stinging jabs. Then he followed this up with a slight half step back and shuffling of his feet further taunting the opponent so they would lose their cool and composure.

Once rattled, for every punch they threw, Flash would give them a flurry of his signature combinations. This was probably how Lapu Lapu was able to lure Magellan to make deadly mistakes. This was exactly how Elorde set up wins over seasoned fighters such as Tanny Campo, Kiyoaki Nakanishi, Cecil Schoonmaker, Tommy Romulo, Hisao Kobayashi, Keiichi Ishikawa, Isarasak Puntainorasing, Kang Il Suh, and Ismael Laguna. He beat Sandy Saddler in a non-title bout while Saddler was the featherweight champion. But the sweetest off them all was when Elorde knocked out defending champion Harold Gomes in the seventh round to win the World super featherweight title in March 1960. He knocked down Gomes seven times during the match.

Elorde's conquest was especially noteworthy since it came 20 years after Philippine-born Ceferino Garcia lost the World middleweight crown and eight years after Filipino American Dado Marino lost the World flyweight title. Filipinos in the Philippines and America were hungry for the bragging rights of a title held by one of their own. Elorde would defend what would eventually become a unified WBC and WBA crown ten times in a span of seven years—one of the longest title reigns in boxing history.

The heart of a true champion

If I [Merino] were to name the best Filipino prizefighter, past and present, I would definitely select Elorde. While Pancho Villa and Ceferino Garcia broke the ice and placed Philippine boxing on the map it could be argued that Elorde polished and brought the sport to another level.

Watching his old videos never ceases to amaze me—his sharp skills, movement and flair. His crisp movements were snappy, from the swift shuffling of his feet to change angles which led to opponents missing their mark, to the way he counters with a blazing sequence of punches exactly describes his ring name "Flash". He truly exemplifies the 1940 DC Comics character.

Manny Pacquiao might be the most decorated and well

paid—if not the highest paid boxer of all time—but I consider him no different from Pancho Villa and Ceferino Garcia who carried devastating punches thrown with an unorthodox style. Elorde was ahead of his time. He had the elusiveness of Filipino flyweight Nonito Donaire Jr. and the stinging one-two combination of American middleweight Sugar Ray Leonard. His shuffling dance-like footwork is comparable to Muhammad "The Greatest" Ali in the mastery of the ring. Most of his fights were characterized with cat and mouse scenarios, building into relentless flurries of exchanges. But let me make a better comparison—Kobe Bryant, Lebron James and many other big names in basketball have their flair, but there is only one Michael Jordan. If Jordan is the master of the basketball court, Elorde is the lord of the ring. Even when he gets into trouble, Flash was always able to adjust and survive the onslaught of combinations from his opponent, and would then turn the situation in his favor.

Growing up as an athlete and a devoted fan of boxing, I used to emulate his moves and end my routine with an inner scream of "FLASH!" He was my idol. I am left with great memories from his fighting days. He was like a super hero, an invincible figure, both inside and outside the ring.

I have read a lot and followed news about him over the years. Some are remarkable stories and others are sad and not so grand. His battle with cancer was a heart wrenching one that some writers were insensitive to. His struggles with the disease had been interpreted as a dysfunction within the

Flash Elorde practicing on the heavy bag in 1959
Photo credit: Tony Triem

family. There were times when he was described as "*pagkain na isusubo na niya ay ipamahagi pa sa iba para di sila magutom*" in English, "food that he was about to put in his mouth he would rather share to the ones who he feels needs it most" like the boy described in Philippine sportswriter Ronnie Nathanielsz' story.

During one of Elorde's routine treatments at a cancer treatment center, it was said that he saw a boy who was also there with the same disease. Touched, the Champ removed his gold crucifix necklace and placed it on the boy's neck, hugged him, and gave him encouragement to keep on fighting and never to forget his faith.

Though Flash was a well-known celebrity, he kept a low-profile. He was not known for inviting the media (press conferences) to showcase his training events. Probably, only a few had seen him in his weakened condition.

Elorde was a champion and advocate for the poor as well. He helped young kids who had aspirations of following his footsteps into the ring. As best described, "Flash Elorde was a consummate gentleman in and out of the ring. He was a good and decent family man. He cared for his children and loved his wife." "Elorde was a kind individual… generous to a fault. As a champion he played by the rules." (Ronnie Nathanielsz, "Remembering 'Flash' Elorde", Philboxing.com, January 3, 2008). He was well known for his charitable contributions and his strong faith in God—a Roman Catholic. Well-liked by most, he showed his love for people. Perhaps the ones who knew him best were accustomed to those acts of kindness.

I was among those lucky ones who had the opportunity to continue to follow the champ after his retirement from the game and before his passing. But at the same time I felt awkward and apprehensive in knowing that my hero had reached a sad state, helpless and weak.

I did not understand then what it took to be suffering from lung cancer, until it hit home when my father–in–law died from it as well. Aside from undergoing the excruciating treatment of the incapacitating disease, he was also dealing with the financial burden that came with it. (Interview with Nonito Donaire Sr., father and boxing training of Nonito Donaire Jr., May 31, 2011)

Flash's pain did not end during retirement. After his death, like that of many other celebrities and celebrated personalities, came the heavy media scrutiny of a life. Rumors sprouted that Elorde, for all his love for humanity, was an exploited pugilist and was taken advantage of by his nationally recognized promoter, Lope "Papa" Sarreal, his father-in-law.

The rumor went that as the champ started winning and earning, his lack of education made him defer decisions to people around him, who exploited him. There were stories that Flash became depressed after he was not allowed to access his winning money. The label "penniless" followed him to his death.

From hindsight and through interviews with people who really knew boxing and the family, Elorde was shown in a different light. He was well cared for and much loved by his in-laws and his family, according to former Olympic boxer Raymundo Fortaleza in an interview on May 31, 2011. His wife, Laura, continues to this day what the Flash started, a humanitarian crusade providing for the poor and giving aid to those less fortunate. This is according to his grandson, Juan Martin Bai Elorde, on May 2005.

My hero, my champ passed away quietly on January 2, 1985. He was just 49 years old.

5

Gentle Ben

"*Kung may tinanim, may aanihin.*"

(If you plant, you will harvest.)

In 1906, the first 15 Filipino laborers recruited by the Hawaiian Sugar Planters Association (HSPA) arrived in the United States. This was the beginning of the Filipino migration to the Hawaiian Islands. The establishment of HSPA recruitment centers in Ilocos Sur and Cebu further increased this number.

By the time Pancho Villa started boxing in the U.S. mainland, there were more than 10,000 Filipinos in Hawaii. By the 1930s, Filipinos had become the largest ethnic group working the vast agricultural plantations, overtaking the Japanese. These first-generation migrants helped plant not just sugar and pineapple but also Filipino boxing sensations in the U.S.

The most famous product of Hawaii's fertile boxing soil is Honolulu-born Salvador "Dado" Marino (October 15,

1915-October 28, 1989). Marino turned professional in 1941 at the age of 26. He would box for more than a decade as a flyweight. The 5'2" Marino had an impressive record 57 wins (21 KO), 14 losses, and three draws in 74 career fights. A highlight of his career was winning the World flyweight title in 1950.

Interestingly, Hawaii has produced three dreaded Filipino American fighters nicknamed "Hawaiian Punch." The first was Waipahu-born Andrew Ganigan (34 wins, 30 by KOs, and 5 losses) who was the North American Boxing Federation (NABF, 1978-1979) and the World Athletic Association (WAA, 1981) lightweight champion as well as *The Ring's* "100 Greatest Punchers."

The second Hawaiian Punch was Ilocos Sur-born Jesus Salud who won an impressive 63 out of 76 bouts, with 38 KOs. Salud's boxing career lasted two decades (1983-2002) culminating in his winning the WBA World super bantamweight title in 1989.

The most recent Fil-Am boxer to adopt the Hawaiian Punch alias is Brian Viloria who had a colorful amateur boxing career winning medals at the National Junior Olympics, National Amateur Championships National Golden Gloves, and the World Amateur Championships. He turned professional in May 2001 and has won the WBC Youth World flyweight title (2002), the WBC light flyweight title (2005), and the IBF light flyweight title (2009).

In this chapter, we feature southpaw Ben Villaflor, a transplant from the Philippine Islands to the Hawaiian Islands, who was a WBA super featherweight (formerly World junior lightweight) champion in the 1970s. Because of his outstanding ring accomplishments, Villaflor is recognized in the following: QTV 11 "*Ang Pinaka Astig Na Pinoy Boxers*" (Top 10 Filipino boxers of All Time); ESPN's "10 Best Filipino fighters"; *The Ring*'s "Greatest Filipino Boxers by Decade"; and *The Ring*'s "The 10 Greatest Filipino Fighters of all-Time".

Villaflor with the three Hawaiian punches—Ganigan, Viloria, and Salud

Photo credit: Robert Abila

Fighting to Support Family

Bienvenido Cajutay Villaflor, nicknamed Ben, was born November 10, 1952 in Hacienda Florentine, Tanjay City in Negros Oriental Province. He had seven brothers and four sisters. His father, Ciriaco Villafor was a laborer from Leyte Province, while his mother, Fermina Cajutay, was a housewife, from Bantayan Island, Cebu Province. Ciriaco and Fermina and their dozen children settled in Barangay Tambanan in the town of Naga in Zamboanga Sibugay Province, one of the poorest municipalities in the Philippines.

Though Villaflor's family was very poor, his parents always stressed the importance of education. His mother stayed home to take care of the children while his father worked at a rubber plantation. Villaflor remembers wearing hand-me-down clothes from his older brothers, going to school and collecting bottles and cans when he was just seven years old, to help with the family finances. At the age of 10, he and his brothers did construction and plantation work as well as odd jobs for neighbors. Despite their poverty, Villaflor and his siblings were always happy, as he stated in our interview on July 21, 2011.

While tapping rubber trees at the plantation when he was 13 years old, Villaflor wondered about a better way to make a living. So he told his brother, Ernesto, who was a professional boxer, if he could come to see him fight. Ernesto agreed but since Villaflor didn't have any money to pay for his admission, he had to wait outside.

As fate would have it, the bout organizers needed a fighter for one card. Villaflor volunteered knowing his parents needed the money. His opponent was about 30 years old and more experienced, but Villaflor won the match convincingly. He gave the purse to his mother to buy clothes and food for the family. From then on, the teenaged Villaflor joined Ernesto every weekend to fight for money. At 15 years old, he and his brother quit school and left home for Manila. They camped out in a broken-down bus waiting for promoters to set up fights for them.

After winning several big matches in Manila, Sad Sam Ichinose, a big-time promoter from Hawaii was impressed by Villaflor's potential and brought him to Honolulu. He was 17 years old then. Given a choice to remain in the Philippines and continue fighting, or to go to Hawaii, he chose to leave because he felt that there would be more opportunities for him to help his family if he was in the U.S.

True enough, with his U.S. winnings, Villaflor was able to send money to help his sister buy a video store, another sister to set up a fruit and vegetable stand, and his brothers to buy a commercial tricycle and a passenger jeepney. He also purchased a fishing boat so his father could earn a living on his own and not have to work for someone else anymore.

Remembering his mother's thoughts on education, Villaflor also sent money home so some of his brothers and sisters could pursue high school and college. Even after retirement from boxing, Villaflor continued to send a portion of his earnings to the Philippines, enabling his family to build a larger home and to buy their own rubber plantation in Zamboanga Sibugay.

While based in Honolulu, Villaflor met and married Denise Molo, a local Hawaiian with Filipino, Irish, Native American, and Chinese ancestries. They met at a Filipino movie house called Zamboanga Theatre in Honolulu. Denise was working the ticket and concession booth at night while attending college during the day.

Enamored by her charming personality, the boxer went to the movie theatre every night to see her. She helped him improve his English and, with her tutoring and inspiration, Villaflor pursued a high school diploma and proceeded to complete an associate's degree at Honolulu Community College. He would adjust his schedule and do his boxer's training during the day and go to college in the evenings.

Villaflor and Denise have three children—Ernestine, Bienvenido II, and Benjamin. They all graduated from college. Bienvenido II tried to follow in his father's footsteps and took up boxing. He seemed to be headed for a promising ring career based on his amateur performances but Villafor dissuaded him from going professional and instead encouraged him to finish college. He followed his father's advice. Villaflor and Molo are blessed with six grandchildren.

Turning professional at thirteen

Villaflor has two nicknames: "Gentle Ben" and "El Torbellino" (The Whirlwind). They seem like contradictory aliases, but they accurately describe his persona outside and inside the ring. He is gentle and soft-spoken to his friends and family but is remembered as a swift and daring slugger by his boxing foes. He idolized his older brother Ernie and Gabriel "Flash" Elorde.

As mentioned earlier, Gentle Ben debuted as a prizefighter when he was only 13 years old, on October 1, 1966, beating Flash Javier by judges' decision in four rounds. Barely over 100 pounds, the teen southpaw would win 12 straight bouts, seven of them by knockouts, before succumbing to an eight-round decision to Roger Boy Pedrano in July 1967. He would lose again to Pedrano in the same fashion two months later. The 5'5" pugilist began the 1970s by drawing with Tony Jumao-As on February 28, 1970 and then going down in defeat by another sad down-to-the-wire decision to Alfredo Avila on May 1, 1970.

Many boxers would have been discouraged by these set-backs but not Villaflor. He reconditioned himself both physically and mentally after these defeats and bounced back by producing an even more remarkable winning streak that lasted two years (1970-1972). This streak was more impressive than the previous one since he carved out 20 wins, five by KOs and eight by TKOs. By then he had become a crowd favorite at both the Araneta Coliseum in Manila and later, the International Center Arena in Honolulu where he competed in 13 contests.

Filipinos in the Philippines celebrated every one of his exciting wins. His newly found extended Filipino American and Hawaiian family in Honolulu beamed with pride as well. His ring demeanor was characterized by sportswriters at that time as "scrappy," "consistent" and "determined".

From his southpaw stance, Villaflor would deliver a stinging straight left and a devastating right which floored many heftier opponents. During his long winning streak, he would defeat seasoned veterans such as Americans Don "Gentleman" Johnson (51-24-3) and Frankie "Irish" Crawford (36-12-4), as well as Venezuelan Alfredo Marcano (35-8-4). It was not an easy climb but the young Villaflor was ambitious and hard-working.

His winning bout with defending champion Marcano earned him his first world title, the WBA World super featherweight championship, in front of wildly cheering fans at the Blaisdell Center in Honolulu on April 25, 1972. He would defend his WBA title for a year. On March 12, 1973, Villafor lost it via points to Japan's Kuniaki Shibata over 15 rounds in Honolulu. Nevertheless, he would regain the coveted title in a rematch with a convincing first-round knockout seven months later.

Gentle Ben would defend the WBA title eight times until August 1976. He defeated the following top-rated challengers from Asia and Latin America: Japan's Takao Maruki (TKO), Yasutsune Uehara (TKO), Morito Kashiwaba (TKO), South Korea's Hyun-Chi Kim (split decision), and Mexico's Rogelio

Villaflor delivers a left hook to his Japanese challenger

Photo credit: Angelo Michael F. Merino

Castaneda (unanimous decision). Villaflor would draw with Japanese Apollo Yoshio, American Ray Lunny III, and Puerto Rican Samuel "El Torbellino" Serrano. Unfortunately, the taller "El Torbellino" would wrest the title from him via a unanimous decision at their October 10, 1976 rematch in San Juan, Puerto Rico.

That was Villaflor's last career bout. He ended with a remarkable 69 total fights: 54 wins (31 KOs), 8 losses, 7 draws. Having started boxing at 13 years old, Lapu Lapu's descendant is certainly entitled to retire comfortably and respectfully at the young age of 23 in the beautiful Hawaiian Islands.

After his retirement from the ring and armed with a college degree, Villaflor worked as the sergeant-at-arms of the Hawaii State Senate and has been there for the last 30 years. In his free time, the former world champion coaches soccer, teaches boxing as a self-defense to high school students, and boxercise fitness classes for adults and seniors.

6

Bad Boy from Dadiangas

"*Ubos-ubos biyaya, pagkatapos nakatunganga.*"
(Spend lavishly and you end up with nothing.)

In the 2008 Beijing Olympics, the proud national flag carrier for the Philippine delegation was a professional boxer—Manny Pacquiao. That scene symbolizes the long-standing irony that exists in Philippine boxing—multiple world-title winners in the professional ranks but no gold medal in the Olympics.

Many have been drawn to emulate the prizefighters featured in this book because of the lure of fame and fortune, foregoing "just" medals and trophies in the amateurs. Jimrex Jaca, Boom Boom Bautista, Bernabe Concepcion, Mark Milligen, among the many, are the *dekada* (decade) 2010s world-class contenders. Not too far away are the young and energetic pugilists of the class of 2020: Mercito Gesta, Edrin Dapudong, and Dodie Boy Peñalosa Jr., who aspires to exceed what his father has accomplished. Why the pros immediately and not the amateurs or the national team first? The answers to these questions are varied, according to the narratives we gathered over the years.

"Contra estilo, pugilato" remarked Enrique Tissert, the Cuban coach who was hired by ABAP for the Beijing Olympics. "Philippine style of boxing is inherently geared towards the demands of pros and not the amateurs—it's about power not points."

"Regionalism," Wally Townsend, Australian trainer and owner of Agoho Tigers Gym in Camiguin Island, Philippines, quipped. "The recruiting for the National team is biased towards the National Capital region. During national competitions, judges are biased towards giving the decision to the boxers that hail from Manila. Why waste your time?"

"Lack of government support for the sport," James Moller, former British promoter, emphasized to us. "Why do public schools have basketball courts and soccer fields? What have these sports done for the Philippines in the last three decades?"

"Disorganized due to politics," was the retort from a high ranking government official. "There are so many governing bodies to this sport and they don't talk to each other—the Philippine Sports Commission, the Philippine Olympic Committee, and the Amateur Boxing Association of the Philippines to name a few."

Ironically, not every professional boxer's life will follow Pancho Villa's or Pacquiao's rags-to-riches pattern. Sometimes the story comes full circle, going from rags-to-riches and then from riches-to-rags. In this chapter, we narrate lessons in and out of the ring from the world champion, Rolando Navarette.

From rags-to-riches

A hard-hitting southpaw, Rolando "Lando" Navarette, is ranked the ninth best super featherweight champion in history by the World Boxing Council. QTV 11's "*Ang Pinaka Astig Na Pinoy Boxers*" (Top 10 Filipino boxers of All Time) and ESPN's "10 Best Filipino Fighters" both honor Navarette's boxing contributions by including him in their lists.

Navarette, born on February 14, 1957, was raised by poor parents in General Santos City (formerly Dadiangas), South Cotabato Province. General Santos is also the hometown of another southpaw and super featherweight champion named Manny Pacquiao. Navarette picked up his ring alias "The Bad Boy from Dadiangas" because of his trademark short temper which made him susceptible to petty fights and brawls from childhood and well into his adulthood.

Like all the male sluggers in this book, Navarette started boxing professionally in his teens. During his first two years (1973-1975) as a professional, the young and ambitious Navarette would fight 17 times and prevail in 13 of them, lose only two, and draw in two bouts. Two interesting highlights from these two years was when he won the Philippines

Games and Amusement Board (GAB) bantamweight title by outpointing Conrado Vasquez in a fight held before his South Cotabato hometown crowd. He would knockout his next two opponents before giving up his GAB title to Fernando Cabanella on October 1, 1975 at the Araneta Coliseum in Quezon City. In June 1977, he vied for the vacant Orient Pacific Boxing Federation bantamweight title against South Korean Yung Shik Kim but did not succeed. This general trend would continue until the end of the year, with him losing three out of five competitions.

The southpaw from General Santos City resurrected himself in the next two years (1978-1980) by winning 10 fights and suffering only one defeat—a fifth round TKO against defending WBC super featherweight champion Alexis "El Flaco Explosivo" Arguello. In May 1981, Navarette challenged Johnny Sato and stripped him of the North American Boxing Federation (NABF) super featherweight title in Honolulu, Hawaii. Five months later, he brought home to the Philippines the biggest prize in pro boxing—a world title. Navarette won the WBC super featherweight title via a convincing fifth round knockout of popular fellow southpaw Ugandan Cornelius Boza Edwards at the championship match held in Toscana, Italy. He flew home to Manila a celebrity with lots of pride and money.

In early 1982, Navarette defended his world title against Korean Choi Chung-II, stopping the pesky challenger in the 11th round of a controversial bout held in Manila. His championship reign was short-lived though since he would lose the WBC belt to Mexican Rafael "Bazooka" Limon in May 1982.

Even in losing, he was still the "Bad Boy" darling of both the media and the movies. Navarette had become so popular that a movie, "Bad Boy from Dadiangas," was released in 1982 with him in the starring role alongside three of the hottest female stars during those times: Amy Austria, Liz Alindogan, and Isabel Rivas. He co-starred in another movie, "Kambal na Kamao" (Twin Fists) alongside former IBF light

A poster of one of Navarette's hit movies with another boxing titlist, Rolando Bohol, IBF flyweight champion

Photo credit: Rolando Navarette Jr.

featherweight champion, Rolando Bohol. Indeed, besides being a boxer, Navarette had also become a movie star.

From riches-to-rags

Navarette was a generous man and spent lavishly on drinking, partying, gambling and women wherever he was. In the mid-1980s, he was accused of rape by a barmaid in Honolulu, found guilty, and sent to prison for four years from 1984-1987. The ex-champ and movie star lost whatever savings he had paying the expensive legal fees.

During his time in prison, his wife abandoned him. Released early on humanitarian grounds, Navarette initiated a comeback beginning in 1988. The Bad Boy from Dadiangas looked like his old self and would come up with a string of eight wins, including getting back at his nemesis, Rafael Limon. But his boxing career took a nosedive thereafter with a series of humiliating losses to unknown prizefighters, so he decided to retire in 1991 with still an impressive 54-15-3, 31 KO record.

The Bad Boy from Dadiangas was supposed to retire quietly in General Santos living on a government stipend, renting out rooms at his boarding house and selling fish at the local market. But because of his short fuse and possibly the onset of Parkinson's disease, heavy drinking and drug abuse, Navarette is prone to being physically violent and verbally abusive, even towards his live-in partners. He has a hard time maintaining relationships and has fathered seven children with different women. Nowadays, the 50+ year old

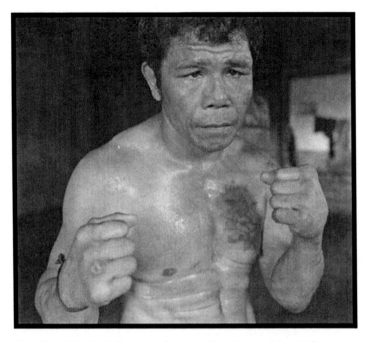

The "Bad Boy" of General Santos City shows his old form
Photo credit: Rolando Navarette Jr.

Navarette still manages to capture the attention of the media but for negative stories. Below are two examples:

On March 24, 2005, Aquiles Zonio of the *Philippine Daily Inquirer* reported:

> On the eve of Manny Pacquiao's match with Mexican fighter Erik Morales in Las Vegas, another boxer from this city went down in shame. Rolando Navarette, a former World Boxing Council junior lightweight champion, lost to a woman, who took just a single

punch to knock him out. On Saturday, at past 9 a.m., Navarette engaged his neighbor, Jennifer Abellanosa, in an argument over a trivial matter in Laray Bagsakan, a drop-off point for farm goods. As tempers flared, Navarette, nicknamed the "Bad Boy from Dadiangas (the former name of this city)," allegedly pushed Abellanosa, who landed flat on the ground. Not contented, the former boxing champ tried to deliver a punch, but Abellanosa managed to grab a steel pipe and, with all her strength, hit him in the head. Navarette staggered before falling to the ground. He tried to get up, but his knees wobbled. He dropped unconscious.

www.abs-cbnnews.com also posted on their interactive news webpage:

On February 14, 2008, Rolando Navarette, "The Bad Boy from Dadiangas" was pronounced out of danger, after being stabbed in the neck by Racman Saliling, a tenant at the boarding house he owns in Bula, General Santos City, using an ice pick. Navarette was also involved in two previous attacks: in 2005, he was hit with a steel pipe by a female neighbor; in 2006, a security guard clubbed his leg with a shotgun at a fish port.

But in a forgiving culture like the Philippines, the jury is still out on the ex-champ, so to speak. His legacy might be from the next generation. After all, one of his sons, Rolando Navarette Jr. is making a name for himself as another member of the class of 2020. He is one of the new breed of Filipino prizefighters.

Though it is still early in his professional career, the younger Navarette has already shown promise with a record of four wins, one loss and three KOs. "J", as his corner calls him, still has a long way to go in sharpening his stuff. Rolando Jr. is a crude southpaw who looks and fights just like his father. One can only hope that he has learned from his father's successes and failures. Rolando Sr. is always seen in his corner giving him moral support and vital instructions during his fights. This may be the best way for Rolando Sr. to redeem himself—to be remembered as a loving and caring father.

7

Original Golden Boy

*"Walang ligaya sa lupa na hindi
dinilig ng luha."*
(There is no earthly bliss not watered by tears.)

At Costco wholesale warehouse in South San Francisco, I [Merino] saw a familiar Filipino face in the produce section washing and drying some fruits and vegetables. I studied him from afar before finally approaching and mustering a greeting, "Champ?" He grinned widely in response. "*Anong ginagawa mo dito* (What are you doing here)," I asked. "*Eto naghahanapbuhay* (just earning a living)," he replied humbly. Our brief encounter ended with an exchange of phone numbers.

Not long before that accidental meeting, I made an offer to Luisito Espinosa, the two-division world champion, to help me coach our student boxers at the University of San Francisco (USF). He accepted my offer graciously and was very enthusiastic and appreciative. The next day, I invited him to come and see our gym and meet our boxers. USF has earned a reputation for its highly competitive university boxing club, so having Espinosa on our coaching staff would be a big boost. Espinosa happily shared with our aspiring pugilists his vast experience and knowledge.

He developed a routine. When his shift ended at Costco, Espinosa, the trainer, would be at USF on Monday, Wednesday, and Friday afternoons until late evenings. Eager faces greeted him every session. They all wanted to learn from the Filipino world champion. With his patient coaching, our boxers improved their competition record and won a number of championships—the National Collegiate Boxing Association's Regional Championship and the Northern California Golden Gloves Championship. I also learned a lot about the ups and downs of his life during the year (2006-2007) Espinosa spent with us.

Navarette's story, in the previous biography, illustrates how easily a rags-to-riches story could turn sour. Espinosa's story is that of a world champion who unfortunately was not able to savor fully the fruits of his hard-earned glory for his country. He is another one of Lapu Lapu's descendants whose career had a sad ending.

His golden years

One of QTV 11 "*Ang Pinaka Astig Na Pinoy Boxers*" (Top 10 Filipino Boxers of All Time), Espinosa is also included in a number of prestigious international lists, such as ESPN's

"10 Best Filipino fighters" and *The Ring*'s "Greatest Filipino Boxers by Decade."

He owned several aliases. One was "Lindol" (or Earthquake) for his earth-shattering punches that rocked his opponent's world whenever they landed. Another was "Golden Boy" for his golden rise to the top of the boxing world, ahead of Oscar de la Hoya. Some sportswriters liked to call him "King Louie." To his Costco colleagues, Espinosa is just Louie, as his name tag indicates. But to our boxer-students at the university, he was respectfully addressed as "Coach."

Luisito Pio Espinosa was born on June 26, 1967 to a poor family in the tough Tondo neighborhood of Manila. He sharpened his boxing skills in the same dilapidated L & M Gym on crowded Paquita Street in Sampaloc, Manila where the then teenage Manny Pacquiao trained and watched the masters including him.

Espinosa turned professional in 1984; his wife Marie Cherie was his trainer, manager, and confidante. Among all the prizefighters in this book, he is probably the best in terms of how quickly he figures out his opponent's weak spots in the ring.

In his first year as a professional boxer, the young 5'7" featherweight built up an 8-2 win-loss record. Not a bad start for the 18-year old novice. He would earn seven more wins in the Philippines leading him to a shot at the WBC International bantamweight title against Mexican Juan Jose Estrada in March 1988. Espinosa would lose by a 10th round TKO before his opponent's jubilant hometown crowd in Tijuana, Mexico.

He regained his confidence after stopping American Mauro Diaz with a quick second-round knockout in San Francisco to win his first international championship, the USA California State bantamweight title. As a side note, this prestigious California boxing title was the same one held by Eleuterio "Little Dado" Zapanta from 1938-1939.

From then on, there was no stopping Espinosa from reaching the top of the boxing world. In 1989, he won the WBA bantamweight title by knocking out Khaokor Galaxy in the first round, before a shocked hometown crowd at the Rajadamnern Stadium in Bangkok, Thailand. He defended the title twice before losing it to Israel Contreras by a fifth-round knockout in 1991. Undeterred, Espinosa annexed another international title in 1993 by winning the vacant WBC Mundo Hispano featherweight title against Mexican Raul Martinez Mora before a sellout crowd in Manila.

In 1995, Espinosa would add another weight division's belt by outpointing Manuel Medina for the WBC featherweight title. He defended the title seven times in four years. Close to 30,000 people came to watch the Golden Boy's July 6, 1996 title defense against Mexican Cesar "La Cobrita" Soto at the historic Luneta Park in Manila. He prevailed in that encounter, but in May 1999, Soto finally succeeded in snatching the WBC belt via a unanimous decision at the Equestrian Center in Texas.

Many of Espinosa's winning bouts were filled with suspense and excitement culminating in early round KOs or TKOs that awed many spectators. The original "Golden Boy" had first-round knockouts of Korean Yong-Man Chun, Thai Thanomchit Kiatkriengkrai, Mexicans Raul Perez and Marco Angel Perez as well as a second-round KO of Colombian Ever Beleno. For these performances, Espinosa won the respect of many American, Latino, and Asian sluggers and the admiration of a global fan base. He was a rock star!

Life turns sour

Espinosa left the Philippines in mid-1998 to campaign in the U.S. and to acquire a permanent residency card, which he was able to secure under the "special skills" category. He began his U.S. boxing career with two convincing wins—against Juan Carlos Ramirez in El Paso, Texas and versus Kennedy McKinney in Indio, California—both in defense of his WBC featherweight title.

According to Espinosa, even though he had attained the status and the acclaim, the promised purse did not come with it. Because of his lack of education, along with his lack of understanding of contracts, his signature on the dotted line got him only broken promises. In short, the two-division titlist claims he was taken for a ride. At times he fought a world title bout on the promise of a big payout and ended up not receiving a penny. Espinosa blamed the members of his camp whom he trusted for the mismanagement of his financial affairs which caused him to go broke and not have the money to support his family. He brought some of them to court but the proceedings were costly in terms of time and money. Moreover, the people he sued were well connected and powerful.

All those worries took a toll on his ring performances. Espinosa went from a winning streak of 12 wins from 1994-1998 to a dismal three wins and six losses from 1999-2005. The last two defeats of his career were to virtual unknowns. Boxingscene.com wrote this post-mortem of his career-ending fight in 2005:

> *At the age of 37, former two-time world champion Luisito Espinosa has lost his ring guile and savvy. Sadly, he seems to have lost his wife and family as well. Marie Cherie, Espinosa's wife, reportedly has recently left his husband…. Aves, a lawyer friend of the boxer, said that Marie Cherie was responsible for ruining her husband's comeback fight that could have led to another title shot.*
>
> *The 5-foot-7 Espinosa prepared hard for 3 months under a new trainer named "Bob," the lawyer added, for his February 18 fight against Mexican Cristobal Cruz at the Stockton Memorial Civic Auditorium in Stockton, California. "Louie trained intensively. The trainer was good and Louie was able to beat up his younger sparring partners," Aves said.*
>
> *"But before he fought on February 18, Cherie called. Once their talk was over, Luisito looked stunned and dazed. He just sat down and would not talk." During the fight,*

Espinosa was a pale shadow of the boxer whose noted ringmanship won him the World Boxing Association bantamweight and World Boxing Council featherweight titles. Ten years Espinosa's junior and a virtual unknown, Cruz dictated the tempo of the match, knocking down the Filipino boxer in the second round before finishing him off in the third.

Not only did Espinosa's finances and focus suffer, so did his personal life. Tired of his empty promises, Marie Cherie left their Las Vegas apartment, taking their three children with her. She eventually left him for good and moved to Texas for another man.

The former champ posing with a training partner
in San Francisco, California

Photo credit: Nonito Donaire Sr.

My last conversations with the two-time world champ were in the fall of 2007. One training day, I got to the gym a bit earlier than usual and found Espinosa looking very depressed. I asked him what was wrong and he answered, "Nothing, coach." I jabbed a few jokes at him to cheer him up but he remained morose. So I told him, "Let us not train today and just talk." He agreed but made me to promise not to say "no" to a very important request he would make.

Thinking that he needed money, I immediately reached for my wallet and told him that whatever I had in my wallet he could have. My gesture made him smile but he said, "*Si coach naman!*" (Coach, please).

"So what then?"

"Okay," he said "But promise me you will listen and give it some serious thought because it would really mean a lot to me."

Espinosa asked me if I would be willing to support him on his comeback. Jokingly, I replied, "You are already here, no need to come back! Why are you leaving?" He said, "No, coach, I am serious! Please train me for about two bouts. This should be enough to pay for a good lawyer so I can collect the money due to me."

Hearing that I felt elated, but at the same time I felt frightened by his plea. It was no ordinary request, it was a tall order. Imagine, a former two-time world champion asking me to train him! Wow! He must have really loved his wife, Marie Cherie to still be that distraught after she left.

Given such an opportunity, other trainers would not have thought twice. But I had to be honest to myself and to Espinosa. I was not confident that that would be the best course to take. First, getting back in the ring at 38 years old would be too difficult; and second, it would take a lot of knowledge and experience on my part to jump from the amateurs to the pros.

An Espinosa comeback had to be planned carefully by a team of experts. After all, people who followed boxing already knew that he had been taken advantaged of before. Most importantly, a team of boxing trainers was necessary to bring him back to world championship form. My inexperience in the professional arena would have only been a disservice to him and his goal; if I accepted, it would have been just out of sympathy.

Just the same, I told him I would give it some really serious thought and would get back to him. I also assured him that whatever my decision, he could count on my help and support. I also told him that if I was able to get a team together, I would not be asking for any compensation. We ended the meeting with a handshake and I told him, "Let us get your family back."

After some research, I learned that Espinosa's license had been suspended. His last scheduled fight with former WBA lightweight champion Lakva Sim was called off after he refused a California State Athletic Commission order to undergo a CT-scan. Golden Boy was officially retired due to "his inability to perform." For his license to be reinstated, he had to undergo the CT-scan and it must come back negative, a normal procedure when a prizefighter is knocked out. For a 38-year-old boxer, it was the most prudent way to go.

I talked to Espinosa about the medical requirement and he explained that he resented doing such a test. He was afraid that the procedure would kill him. He thought there was a conspiracy for him not to fight again because "they know I can still fight for the championship."

"*Ayaw na nila akong bigyan ng pagkakataun, coach* (They do not wish to give me a chance)." "*Natatakot akong mamatay sa loob ng CT-scan* (I am afraid to die inside the CT-scan)." I continued to explain to Espinosa that this was a routine preventive medical procedure and without it, he would not be allowed to box professionally. He kept quiet and just looked at the floor for almost an hour. I worried that he had become delusional and needed psycho-social help.

Espinosa never returned to our gym again.

Days, months and years passed, and I would only hear of Espinosa from some articles in Philippine newspapers and on the internet. Recently, I heard he was back in the Philippines seeking assistance from Manny Pacquiao to either endorse him to fight again or to help him recover the large sum of money that was not paid him. Espinosa, a descendant of Lapu Lapu, ended his ring career with a respectable 47-13-0, 26 KOs record.

8

Brothers in the Ring

"Matibay ang walis, palibhasa'y magkabigkis."
(A broom is sturdy because its strands are tightly bound.)

As a competitive American boxing university, the University of San Francisco has generously hosted the Amateur Boxing Association of the Philippines (ABAP) team over the years to help expose them to some of the San Francisco Bay Area's finest pugilists and coaches. During their 2010 visit, the ABAP roster listed two athletes whose last name was "Saludar." We asked Executive Director Ed Picson if there was a mistake. Ed replied, "No, the two boxers—Rey and Victorio—are *magkapatid* (brothers). They are the pride of South Cotabato." This fact immediately reminded us of the four famous Fortaleza boxing brothers who have made the Philippines proud in the amateur ranks – Ricardo, Reynaldo,

Renato, and Rogelio. But we learned that there are stellar siblings in Philippine professional boxing too.

Sometimes the ties that bind siblings lead them to parallel destinies in the ring. This is what we discovered in our research and observations. Since the days of Lapu Lapu, siblings have worked together for the same causes—Jose and Paciano Rizal, Andrés and Procopio Bonifacio, Juan and Antonio Luna, as well as Jose and Rafael Palma. Their common quest for Philippine freedom from Spain fueled their connected passions.

Similarly, in professional boxing, a number of siblings have joined the many driven by glory, titles and money. There were the half brothers, Pancho Villa and Little Pancho, and the fearsome Flores brothers—Macario, Francisco, Irineo, and Elino. Born and bred in New Orleans, Louisiana, were the half Filipino, half Creole Docusen brothers – Bernard and Maxie, alias "Big Duke" and "Little Duke," respectively. Transplants from General Santos City, South Cotabato to San Leandro, California are the Donaire brothers – Glenn aka "The Filipino Bomber" and Nonito Jr. aka "The Filipino Flash." There was also Ernesto, Ben Villaflor's brother. Manny Pacquiao's younger brother, Bobby alias "The Sniper," was also a prizefighter. Bobby held national and regional titles as a pro.

In this chapter, we focus on the lives of the explosive Peñalosa boxing brothers—Dodie Boy, Gerry, and Jonathan—who have distinguished themselves in the ring by collectively winning many national, regional, and international titles. The oldest of the siblings, Dodie Boy, was both an IBF light flyweight champion and an IBF flyweight champion. His younger brother, Jonathan, held the WBC International flyweight title. Their youngest brother, Gerry, was both a WBC super flyweight titlist and a WBO bantamweight titlist. All three Peñalosa brothers were generous about sharing their knowledge and talents to the next generation of Philippine champions by dispensing valuable advice, promotional support, training tips, and holding technical clinics, from the *barangay* (village) level all the way to the national level.

Growing up in a boxing family

Dodie Boy, Gerry, and Jonathan were all born and raised in San Carlos City, Negros Occidental Province. Pancho Villa, Small Montana, and Little Dado also came from the same province. Diosdado or "Dodie Boy" was born on November 19, 1962, Jonathan on May 6, 1967, and Geronimo or "Gerry" on August 7, 1972.

Two other brothers, Carlos Jr. and Carmelo, were national amateur boxing standouts. It is not surprising that the brothers took up boxing because their father, Carlos "Carl" Peñalosa Sr. (10 wins, 12 losses, 6 draws) was also a professional slugger as well as their uncle Ricardo "Ric" Peñalosa (13 wins, 6 losses, 5 draws). Carlos Sr. was both Philippine national lightweight and light welterweight GAB champion in the 1960s. The brothers had the right pedigree.

Their mother, Dolores Jumaral, was from General Santos City. She raised her five frisky boys and a daughter, Marissa, to be caring and supportive of each other. Thus, when Dodie Boy won his first IBF world championship belt, he used part of the purse to purchase a larger family home in Cebu City where the entire family stayed.

Now, the Peñalosa brothers are proud and attentive parents. Dodie Boy Peñalosa and wife Marie Ann Pumar-Peñalosa have three children. Their two sons, Dodie Boy Jr. and Dave, are both professional boxers, the third-generation Peñalosa brothers to become prize fighters. Jonathan Peñalosa and his wife, Tata Rodriguez-Peñalosa, have four kids, a son and three daughters. Gerry Peñalosa and his wife, Goody Lledo-Peñalosa, have a son and a daughter.

Dodie Boy Sr., the father, corners for his son, Dodie Boy Jr.
Photo credit: Dodie Boy Peñalosa Jr.

All three, Dodie Boy, Jonathan, and Gerry Peñalosa are southpaws. But that is where their similarities ended. Dodie Boy combines counter punching and risky brawling styles. Jonathan is a careful, classic counter puncher. Gerry is the most technical and methodical pugilist among the three. The Peñalosa brothers are often seen together watching other upcoming Filipino boxers' professional bouts. They are generous with their ring advice as well as financial assistance to those in need. So it was not surprising when they agreed that part of the purse for Gerry's last career fight in Zamboanga City against Thailand's Yodsaenkeng "The Robot" Kietmangmee would be donated to compatriot Z Gorres, who suffered a career-ending brain injury from his last fight.

Diosdado "Dodie Boy" Peñalosa Sr. (31 wins, 7 losses, 2 draws, 13 KOs)

Dodie Boy's rise was phenomenal—18 wins, zero defeats in four straight years (February 1982 - February 1986). This was notwithstanding the fact that he was afflicted with polio at birth. Undaunted by his physical disability, the ruthless southpaw picked up national, regional and international titles during his winning stretch.

Dodie Boy started out by winning the Philippine lightweight championship on November 26, 1982 with a twelfth-round stoppage of Romy Austria. Four months later, he gains the OPBF light flyweight title with an eleventh-round

TKO of Sung Nam Kim. Then he became the first IBF light flyweight champion in December 1983 with a seventh-round TKO win over Satoshi Shingaki who would later become the inaugural IBF bantamweight champion. He defended his IBF world title three times before vacating the belt.

In 1986, he moved up weight division to challenge the WBA flyweight champion Hilario Zapata but lost. Peñalosa captured his second world crown the following year with a convincing fifth round knockout of IBF flyweight defending champion Hi Sup Shin. Unfortunately, he lost the belt in his first defense to Chang-Ho Choi. Dodie Boy would continue to fight until August 1995 and formally retired from competitive ring boxing at the end of the year. In 2009, along with his two brothers he joined the training team of Nonito Donaire Jr. The team helped Nonito Jr. defeat Raul Martinez in Donaire's third title defense of his IBF flyweight championship, a belt Dodie Boy once held in 1987.

Geronimo "Gerry" Peñalosa (55 wins, 8 losses, 2 draws, 37 KOs)

Gerry turned pro in 1989, had the longest career, the highest number of wins, and the most number of KOs among the Peñalosa brothers. Future Hall of Famer and long-time Pacquiao trainer Freddie Roach and Philippine boxing aficionados all observed that Gerry was probably one of the most technically sound Filipino pugilists.

The 5'4" boxer was a smart slugger, a superb counter puncher who had excellent footwork as well as an iron jaw. All of these characteristics combined gave the southpaw from Negros Occidental the distinction of never being knocked out in his entire boxing career, which ran until 2010 when he retired.

The youngest of the three Peñalosa siblings out did his eldest brother's phenomenal winning stretch with an equally remarkable 19 bouts, from May 1989 to June 1992. In his ninth fight, he outclassed Indonesian Rachmat to win the vacant IBF Inter-Continental light flyweight title. After losing the Philippine GAB bantamweight title fight to Samuel Duran in August 1992, he would come up with 20 straight wins. He

A victorious Gerry Peñalosa celebrates.
Photo credit: Dodie Boy Peñalosa Jr.

captured the WBC super flyweight title with a decision win over Hiroshi Kawashima on February 27, 1997. He defended the title three times.

After a series of setbacks which made him decide to take a two-year hiatus, a more focused Gerry came back in November 2004 and defeated Bangsaen Sithpraprom for the lightly regarded World Boxing Foundation super flyweight title in Manila. In March 2007, he would lose an attempt to gain the unified International Boxing Association (IBA) super bantamweight title-WBO super bantamweight title against Mexican southpaw Daniel Ponce de Leon. But five months later, Gerry gained his second world title by knocking out Jhonny Gonzalez in the seventh round of the WBO bantamweight championship at the Arco Arena in Sacramento, California. Eastsideboxing.com contributing sports writer, Carlo Pamintuan narrated how the feisty Peñalosa beat the odds:

> The younger fighter appeared to be in control of the match in the early rounds, as he skillfully kept the much shorter Peñalosa away with crisp jabs. Peñalosa stayed patient and continued to walk forward even though he is getting hit by some of the Mexican's punches. In the seventh round, Peñalosa got an opportunity, when Gonzalez launched a strong right that missed Peñalosa's head. Gonzalez failed to pull his arm back quickly

and at that short moment, leaving a hole for the veteran fighter, who then threw a precise and solid left hook to Gonzalez' body. The defending champion fell on the canvas a few moments after receiving the counter-attack; the Mexican tried to get up and fight again but failed to do it, [he] remained down on the canvas.

The 35-year-old descendant of Lapu Lapu proudly brought home another world championship—making his record two titles in two weight divisions. This win allowed him to equal his elder brother, Dodie Boy's feat.

Jonathan Peñalosa (15 wins, 4 losses, 1 draw, 7 KOs)

Jonathan is the least known of the Peñalosa brothers, probably because he only fought for eight years (November 1985–December 1993) but never won a world title. We would like to accord him better recognition in this chapter as part of the Peñalosa triumvirate.

Record-wise, the "middle brother" is almost toe-to-toe with his more famous siblings, also producing quite an enviable start—a string of 15 wins and 1 draw, from 1985 to 1991. During this six-year run, the southpaw knocked out half of his opponents. The most significant of the wins occurred in October 1989 when Jonathan won the vacant WBC International flyweight title via a first-round TKO over Kyoto, Japan-based Emil Romano Matsushima. He defended it successfully five months later against Toshio Aikawa in front of thousands of Filipinos at the Araneta Coliseum in Quezon City. The bout ended in a fourth-round knockout.

On his seventeenth bout in March 1992, Jonathan vied for the WBA flyweight title against Yong-Kang Kim in Incheon, South Korea. Unfortunately, he was knocked out in the sixth round. After that, he suffered three disappointing losses which led to his decision to retire in 1993.

Since then, Jonathan has concentrated on supporting his brothers' and other upcoming boxers'dreams. In 2009, he joined Dodie Boy as part of Team Donaire and shuttles between Manila and Team Donaire's training camp at the Undisputed Boxing Gym in San Carlos, California, and wherever Donaire has a bout.

What is life after professional boxing for them? Since 2006, Dodie Boy Peñalosa Sr. has been working at the Cebu City Hall as the head coach of the Cebu amateur boxing team. He is also quite busy conducting *barangay* boxing clinics, a grassroots recreational and fitness project of the Cebu City sports commission.

Jonathan and Gerry Peñalosa are both based in Manila. After almost a decade in the ring, Jonathan retired to become a professional trainer and coach. Gerry, who retired in 2010, focused on being a promoter-trainer. His stable includes nephew, Dodie Boy Jr. He also co-manages with his brother Carmelo the Peñalosa Boxing Gym in Mandaluyong City where Manny Pacquiao trained for his fight with Miguel Cotto for the WBO welterweight title.

9

Filipino Flash

"Ang hindi marunong magmahal sa sariling wika, daig pa ang malangsang isda."
(He who does not love his national language is worse than a smelly fish.)

Even though Nonito "Filipino Flash" Donaire Jr.'s boxing career is far from ended, we decided to include him in this compilation because of his already exemplary accomplishments.

Donaire is a three-division world champion, winning five world titles in three different boxing weight classes. Presently, he is the WBC and WBO Bantamweight World Champion. In August 2011, *The Ring* magazine rated Donaire as the number three pound-for-pound boxer in the world and the number one bantamweight boxer.

Besides his WBC and WBO titles, the Filipino Flash has held the WBA super flyweight interim title, IBF flyweight title, and IBO flyweight title. Early in his career, Donaire also won the WBO Asia Pacific flyweight title and the North American Boxing Federation (NABF) super flyweight title and later on, the WBC Continental Americas bantamweight title. Like Ana Julaton and Manny Pacquiao, Donaire's story is still unfolding. Thus, what we provide here is a snapshot.

Training with his father and brother

Nonito Gonzales Donaire Jr., also known to his family and close friends as Junjun, was born on November 16, 1982 in Talibon, Bohol. He is the third among the five children of Nonito Donaire Sr. and Imelda Gonzales. Along with his two brothers and two sisters, Donaire was raised in General Santos City, South Cotabato, where they attended the same elementary school where the eight-division world champion Manny Pacquiao went to. His father, Nonito Sr., started out as a tricycle driver and then found a better and more stable job with the Philippine Army where he worked for eight years (1982-1990). Petitioned by his siblings, Nonito Sr. immigrated to the United States in 1990 and was joined by the rest of the family in 1991, settling in San Leandro, a suburb of San Francisco in Northern California.

To shield them from the temptation of joining local Filipino gangs, Nonito Sr. decided to enroll the junior Donaire and his brother, Glenn, at the U.S. Karate and Boxing Gym in

Hayward, a city adjacent to where they lived. Initially, Donaire Jr. became more engrossed with the karate classes while the father taught his older brother how to box. Nonito Sr. had learned to box at the gyms in General Santos City and had fought some amateur bouts, including when he was with the army. He recalls that the best sparring partners those days where the drunk men on the streets of General Santos who were always picking fights. When the young Donaire saw his older brother bringing home boxing trophies and awards from local competitions, he decided that he was going to shift from karate to boxing. He asked his father to train him alongside his brother.

The Donaire brothers, Glenn and Nonito Jr., and their proud father-trainer, Nonito Sr.
Photo credit: Nonito Donaire Sr.

During those days, Nonito Jr. and Glenn would spar, and the younger one would often be beaten. As kids, the brothers watched fight films of Julio Cesar Chavez, Oscar dela Hoya, Felix Trinidad, and Nonito Jr.'s hero, Nicaraguan featherweight Alexis Argüello. According to him, it was from watching Argüello that he picked up how to increase the power and speed in his left hook. There were no Manny Pacquiao YouTube videos to watch and emulate then.

With consistent and rigorous training from their father, the brothers were able to sharpen their techniques. While going to high school in San Lorenzo, the city next to San Leandro, the Donaire brothers would proudly bring home an assortment of regional and district amateur boxing championships. Eventually, the Bohol-born Filipino American prizefighter would compete in bigger competitions and win three national championships: the National Silver Gloves in 1998, National Junior Olympics in 1999, and the National USA Tournament in 2000. He also won the International Junior Olympics in 1999. His amateur record was an impressive 68-8 with 5 TKOs.

The road to three-division titles

Losing in their qualifying attempt for the U.S. Olympic boxing team became a turning point in the life and career of both Nonito Jr. and his brother, Glenn. So even with a scholarship offer in Michigan, they told their father-trainer and mother that they would like to turn professional. Their parents were hesitant at first since they wanted their sons to go to college. But the brothers convinced them that boxing is their passion and their favored career. Nonito Sr. and Imelda relented and gave their blessings.

In 2000, Nonito Jr. and Glenn signed up with manager Jackie Kallen who convinced the family to move to Los Angeles to widen their exposure and opportunities. Nonito Jr. was able to fight four professional bouts, winning three of them, but Kallen had a hard time getting them in cards because, according to her, "No one wants to watch Filipino fighters. Promoters are more interested in Mexican boxers." This was before Manny "Mexicutioner" Pacquiao came to town.

Frustrated, Nonito Sr. decided to move his family back to General Santos City on November 16, 2001, Nonito Jr.'s 19th birthday. The father got the boys licensed in the Philippines and had them fight professionally.

While based in the Philippines, Nonito Jr. fought three professional bouts within a year and gained his first regional title by defeating Thailand's Kaichon Sor Vorapin for the vacant WBO Asia Pacific flyweight title at the University of Guam in September 2002. He knocked out the future world title challenger in the second round. His career was on the verge of peaking but the family decided to do another training move and returned to their old San Leandro home base in 2003. Donaire Sr. was convinced that, together with fame and glory in the Philippines, would come the dangerous combination of drugs, alcohol, and women. The lessons from the Bad Boy from Dadiangas and other fallen champs were definitely in his mind.

With a more permanent U.S.-based training camp, Nonito Jr. trained hard and won seven straight matches leading to a clash with Armenian American Kahren Harutyunyan for the vacant NABF super flyweight title on January 20, 2006. The Filipino Flash prevailed in a split decision and annexed his second international regional championship. He successfully defended his NABF title against the veteran Oscar Andrade from Mexico. With those wins, he started to get the attention of fight promoters. Nonito Donaire Jr. was ready for the big leagues.

Another critical turning point in his career happened on July 7, 2007 when Donaire Jr. was matched up as a 7-1 underdog, against Australian Armenian Vic "The Raging Bull" Darchinyan, who was then undefeated in 28 outings. With his trademark lightning moves, he knocked out Darchinyan in the fifth round, winning the International Boxing Federation (IBF) and International Boxing Organization (IBO) flyweight world titles. This victory was awarded *The Ring*'s "Knockout of the Year" and "Upset of the Year." The Filipino Flash had his first world championship. He also avenged his older brother's loss to Darchinyan the previous year.

From 2008-2009, Donaire Jr. successfully defended his IBO and IBF flyweight titles against seasoned fighters: Mexico's Luis "Titi" Maldonado (35-2-1 record), South Africa's Moruti "Baby Face" Mthalane (23-1-0 record), and Texas' Raul

"The Cobra" Martinez (24-0-0). In his defense against Martinez in front of thousands of cheering *kababayans* (countrymen) at the Araneta Coliseum in Quezon City, Philippines, Donaire Jr. scored a TKO after 2:42 into the 4th round.

With his impressive victories, Donaire Jr. was included for the first time in *The Ring*'s pound-for-pound rankings. He replaced his father as his trainer in Team Donaire with the Peñalosa brothers—Dodie Boy and Jonathan. He also moved to a new training facility at the Undisputed Boxing Gym in San Carlos, California. On August 8, 2008, Donaire Jr. took time off from his busy schedule to marry his biggest supporter, Rachel Marcial, a Filipino American USA National Collegiate and Military Taekwondo Champion.

Trainer Jonathan Peñalosa with the three-division champ, Donaire

Photo credit: Ronnie Lu

Four months after his Martinez victory, he set his sights on a second-divisional championship—the interim WBA super flyweight title. He gained the belt in a 12-round unanimous decision against Panama's Rafael "El Torito" Concepcion (13-3-1 record) who had stepped in to replace Mexico's Hugo Fidel Cazares, his original opponent. The Filipino Flash dedicated his fight against Concepcion in memory of late Philippine President Corazon "Cory" Aquino who had then just passed away. He made a special request to Everlast to provide him with a yellow robe with the inscription "I. M. O. (in memory of) former President Cory Aquino."Two days after the win, he arrived in Philippines, where he was feted with a grand motorcade by Manila Mayor Alfredo Lim.

In December 2010, Donaire Jr. challenged former WBA bantamweight champion Vladimir Sidorenko for the vacant WBC Continental Americas Bantamweight title. He knocked down the Ukranian champion thrice, becoming the first man to stop Sidorenko. The win opened up the chance to face Mexican veteran Fernando "Cochulito" Montiel (44-2-2 record).

In February 2011, Donaire Jr. stopped Montiel with a second-round TKO to win both the World Boxing Council (WBC) and World Boxing Organization (WBO) bantamweight titles. Midway into round two, he took a right to the head from Montiel, then immediately countered with a stinging left to the head that sent Montiel crumpling to the canvas. Montiel rose to continue but Donaire Jr. rushed over to land a left and a right. At that point, referee Russell Mora waived both arms to halt the fight.

With this glorious victory, Donaire Jr. became only the second Filipino (Pacquiao was the first) to become a three-division world champion. In every fight, he proudly wears the colors of his Filipino heritage, never forgetting his humble beginnings.

On February 28, 2011, the Philippine Senate formally adopted two resolutions congratulating and commending Lapu Lapu's descendant for being an outstanding Filipino boxer and for bringing honor and pride to the republic. Like Filipina American Ana Julaton, who we will talk about in the next chapter, Donaire adores both his homelands—the Philippines and the U.S.

10

Fearless Filipinas

"Sa taong walang takot, walang mataas na bakod."
(To a fearless person, no fence is too high.)

Lapu Lapu's pedigree produced many fearless women fighters for freedom. There were Melchora "Tandang Sora" Aquino who was the nurse and mother of the revolution; Gabriela Silang who, after her husband's death, took over the leadership of his insurgent group; Marcela Agoncillo who sewed the first Philippine flag, among others. Aquino, Silang, and Agoncillo were not boxers but, in their own way, they helped deliver the necessary knockout punch that gave birth to the Republic.

Women competing in boxing matches were not taken seriously in the past, both in the Philippines and the United States. It was only in the last 40 years when women were able to compete in U.S. amateur boxing. And only between

1975 to 1978 did the states of Nevada, California, and New York begin issuing boxing licenses that allowed women to compete professionally.

The first four-card bout was held at the University of Minnesota in May 1978. The following year, the first all-female professional boxing card was held at the Los Angeles Sports Arena. But it took U.S. Amateur Boxing more than a decade to finally amend their by-laws, allowing women pugilists to compete. Lawsuits and protests had to happen. And in 1996, women's boxing got a publicity boost when light middleweight champ Christy "The Coal Miner's Daughter" Martin graced the cover of the April 15, 1996 issue of *Sports Illustrated*. That same year, the United Kingdom lifted its ban on women boxing. Finally, after a long wait, women's amateur boxing will make its debut at the 2012 Olympic Games in London.

Since these milestones, a number of international sanctioning bodies for women's professional boxing have emerged, including the Women's International Boxing Association (WIBA), the Women's International Boxing Federation (WIBF), the International Women's Boxing Federation (IWBF), and the International Female Boxers Association (IFBA). The World Boxing Association (WBA), World Boxing Organization (WBO), and World Boxing Council (WBC) also sanction women's professional boxing predominantly in North and South America.

Inspired by these international events, in 2006, the Games and Amusement Board (GAB), the regulatory body for professional sports in the Philippines amended its by-laws, paving the way for Filipina boxers to be licensed to compete for pay, locally and internationally. Since these global milestones, more and more Philippine-born and American-born Filipina prizefighters are appearing on the rankings and cards of regional and international sanctioning bodies. Indeed, the world of boxing is evolving.

Two-time world champion Ana Julaton is the main feature of this chapter. A fearless Filipina who stormed into professional boxing in the late 2000s, she is literally a "hurricane" among the Pacific storms in this book. Following Julaton in terms of boxing accomplishments are WIBA minimumweight champion Gretchen "Chen Chen" Abaniel, WIBA flyweight champion Elena "Baby Doll" Reid, and WIBF junior straw-weight champion Sarah "Thrilla from Manila" Goodson. The unfolding stories of these fearless Filipina boxers make them worthy of being in the company of the outstanding Filipino boxers in this book.

Ana "The Hurricane" Julaton (9 wins, 2 losses, 1 draw, 1 KO)

Named one of the "100 Most Influential Filipinas in the USA, Luciana Bonifacio Julaton was born on July 5, 1980 at Saint Luke's Hospital in San Francisco, California. Her parents are Cesario Julaton, Jr., from Pozorrubio, Pangasinan Province and Amelia Bonifacio from Masantol, Pampanga Province. Julaton's father immigrated to the U.S. in 1959 while her mother came in 1975. She has a younger brother,

Cesario III. Ana, to her friends and family, grew up not too far away from the "Lipi ni Lapu Lapu" mural in the South of Market (SOMA) neighborhood of San Francisco. Interestingly, another Filipina American warrior was raised in the same area—Victoria Manalo Draves—who was an Olympic gold medalist in platform diving.

Julaton has great memories of Russ Street across from Bessie Carmichael School in SOMA. Life was simple. Besides her parents, she lived with her grandparents, great grandpa, aunties, and uncles. She remembers having *champorado* (chocolate porridge) and *pandesal* (bread rolls) for breakfast and walking across the street to go to school. After school, she would hang out with her older cousins who lived nearby and played outside until her father picked her up after he finished work. The family moved from San Francisco, to Pacifica, to Vallejo, and eventually settled in Daly City. Julaton graduated from El Camino High School and the City College of San Francisco.

Julaton is relatively new to boxing having started only in 2004. But she is not new to combative sports since her father made her train in martial arts when she was little. It was only while working as a bok-fu instructor at the West Wind Martial Arts and Boxing School in Berkeley, California, that Julaton was introduced to boxing through a lecture session organized by her trainer-manager, Angelo Reyes. She continues to teach bok-fu to kids at West Wind.

Nicknamed "The Hurricane," the long-haired

Julaton is the first American and Filipino American boxer to simultaneously hold both the Women's WBO super bantamweight title and the WIBA super bantamweight title. But before storming into the pros, Julaton paid her dues in the amateur ranks compiling more than thirty amateur bouts under her belt. Before turning professional in 2007, she was ranked second among all female amateur pugilists in the United States.

We witnessed Julaton compete as a budding amateur during the 2005 and 2006 editions of our University of San Francisco (USF) Hilltop Cup, which annually draws the best male and female boxers from all over the San Francisco Bay Area and beyond. The beautiful pugilist fights like a Filipino woman scorned—full of passion and inertia. Cognizant of her beginnings on our campus, Julaton continues to come to USF to spar with Philippine team female sluggers as well as grace our yearly Hilltop Cup.

Julaton made her amateur boxing debut in 2004, winning a silver medal at the San Francisco Golden Gloves competitions despite having formally trained for only two weeks. After delivering a good performance at the U.S. National Golden Gloves in 2005, she trained with two-division world champion Carina Moreno and trainer Rick Noble, further improving her style and technique.

By 2007, Julaton, hoping for a shot to represent her American homeland internationally, joined the unsuccessful campaign to include women's boxing at the 2008 Beijing

Olympics. Frustrated by the outcome and the politics involved, she decided to just turn professional. She was scheduled to make her debut against Hondi Hernandez as part of the undercard for the Pacquiao-Barrera rematch in October 2007. Team Julaton turned to Team Pacquiao's lead trainer, Freddie Roach, at the Wild Card Gym in Los Angeles. She impressed the future hall of famer with her serious work ethic and so Roach exposed the aspiring female pugilist to some of his best male boxers to prepare her well for Hernandez.

But Julaton faced disappointment again when her fight was canceled because Hernandez failed to make the weight limit. Finally, the following month, she fought Canada-born Margherita "Stallionette" Valentini (6 wins-5 losses-0 draw record) at the Morongo Casino Resort and Spa, Cabazon, California. By nightfall, the San Francisco-born Filipina had gained her first pro win with a convincing unanimous decision.

In August 2008, the 5'5" Julaton had a four-win, zero-loss, and one-draw record going into the bout against Dominga Olivo (6-4-1 record) for the vacant WBC International female super bantamweight title at the Tachi Palace Hotel and Casino in Lemoore, California. The more experienced prizefighter from Brooklyn, New York would win the world title in a heartbreaking split decision after eight rounds of slugging.

After the loss, Julaton regained her composure, trained harder and faced an even higher mountain a year later. The Hurricane went up against the veteran Kelsey "Road Warrior" Jeffries, who had an impressive 41-9-1 record. The fight was the main event of the "American Metal and Irons' Fight Night" at the Tank in San Jose, California. At stake, was the vacant International Boxing Association female super bantamweight title. In a ten-round stop-go battle, the Hurricane's speedy and lethal left jabs sneaking in from the outside allowed her to pull off a hard-earned majority decision (MD) win versus the Road Warrior who was not as effective with her trademark inside attacking style. The underdog from San Francisco could not believe she had become a world champion. It happened in just five bouts—one of the fastest ascension to a world title in the history of professional boxing.

Three months later, the Hurricane would stake her title and go after the vacant WIBA super bantamweight title against another veteran Donna "Nature Girl" Biggers from South Carolina who had an intimidating 19-8-1 record, with 16 KOs. To prepare for her first title defense, Julaton asked Nonito Donaire Sr., father of world champion Nonito Donaire Jr., to join her team as her lead trainer. Team Julaton successfully helped her defend their newly acquired world title by pulling off a unanimous decision win over Donna Biggers. She also became the inaugural World Boxing Organization super bantamweight female champion.

In March 2010, Julaton tried for a record third world title against the seasoned Lisa "Bad News" Brown (16-4-3 record) for the vacant WBA junior featherweight title. Unfortunately, she was outscored in a unanimous decision against the gritty southpaw from Trinidad and Tobago. Since the loss to Brown,

Julaton has had three straight victories defending her WIBA and WBO world super bantamweight titles.

Besides Manny Pacquiao, the fearless Filipina's boxing idols are Joe Louis, Ray Leonard, and Alexis Arguello. Because of her successes, Julaton has become the darling of the Philippine, Filipino American, Asian American, and the mainstream U.S. media. In spite of her stardom, the Hurricane continues to be very humble, respectful, grateful and focused. We last saw her at West Bay Pilipino Multi-Services Center, a non-profit social service organization in San Francisco's South of Market neighborhood, where she grew up. The Hurricane was signing autographs and entertaining poor, at-risk Filipino kids. We could not help but wonder who among the giggly girls might just follow their *Ate* (elder sister) Ana's footsteps.

Julaton gives back to community by spending time with girls from her old South of Market neighborhood
Photo credit: Rudy Asercion

Gretchen "Chen Chen" Abaniel (10 wins, 2 losses, 0 draws, 2 KOs)

Our second fearless Filipina is five-footer Gretchen Magbanua Abaniel. Nicknamed Chen Chen, Abaniel was born on November 4, 1985 in far-flung Barangay Langogan, Puerto Princesa City, Palawan Province. She is the pride and joy of this remote Philippine province.

Abaniel is the daughter of Filemon Abaniel Jr., a *barangay* (village) official, and Perla Magbanua a *sari-sari* (convenience) store owner. She is the second child and only girl among three siblings. Her older brother is Raymond and younger brother is Ian.

Since her elementary school days, Abaniel was always involved in sports. She started out in the track team and then moved on to volleyball, basketball, and karate-do in high school. Her father taught her karate but his co-worker introduced her to some boxing.

Abaniel's formal entry into the boxing ring was somewhat accidental. Her father had asked her to accompany her younger brother Ian, an aspiring amateur boxer, who wanted to compete at a boxing tournament in a neighboring barangay. Her brother was not able to find a matching opponent but there was one who was willing to fight Abaniel. This was the beginning of her amateur bouts which took the young pugilist from Palawan all over the country. After many impressive wins, she was selected to train with the elite Philippine national team in 2003. She represented the Philippines for three years and was mentored by Olympic silver medalist Roel Velasco.

Together with Ana Julaton, Abaniel was honored at the 2011 Gabriel "Flash" Elorde Memorial Annual Boxing Awards and Banquet of Champions. She turned professional in 2006 and debuted at the EXPO Garden Hotel in Kunming, China, winning by decision over hometown favorite, Li Hai Li. Less than a year later, she defeats Li again for the WIBA Asia-Pacific minimumweight title. In 2007, during a span of just nine months, Abaniel fought and won five straight contests including another international championship belt—the vacant WBC International minimumweight title—by defeating Thailand's Lilly Kekietgym in Manila. However, four months later, in March 2008, Abaniel experienced disappointment when she lost a controversial hometown decision against Chon-Rong Son for the WBA minimumweight title.

On March 25, 2009, the tiny but gritty Filipina won another title when she annexed the vacant WIBA minimumweight belt by defeating the tough Nongbua Lookprai-aree from Thailand. The orthodox boxer from Puerto Princesa would defended it successfully a year later against Thailand's Fahpratan Looksaikongdin and Nongbua Lookprai-aree before losing it to their veteran compatriot Samson Tor Buamas (19 wins, 2 losses record) in February 2011.The pride and joy of Palawan is trained by former Australian pugilist Terry Mogg. Her boxing idols include Manny Pacquiao, Onyok Velasco, Roel Velasco, Gerry Peñalosa, and Floyd Mayweather.

Still drenched in sweat, Abaniel, the WIBA world
champ after the title bout

Photo credit: Gretchen Abaniel

Elena "Baby Doll" Reid (19 wins, 6 losses, 6 draws, 5 KOs)

Filipino American Elena Y'lugto Reid is the third among our fearless Filipinas. She was born in Phoenix, Arizona on November 1st, 1981. Her father, Kyle Reid Sr., is a former U.S. Navy serviceman from Phoenix while her mother, Rose Y'lugto is a nurse originally from Santa Cruz, Laguna Province in the Philippines. She has an older sister, Donna, and two younger brothers, Kyle Jr. and Vicente. Her boxing influences are Cornelius Boza Edwards, Shane Mosley, Mike Tyson, and her University of Nevada, Las Vegas (UNLV) boxing coach, Chris Ben.

A 5'2" southpaw, Reid is nicknamed "Baby Doll" for her pretty doll-like face and petite size. But there is nothing doll-like about this Filipino American slugger since she is both a professional boxer and mixed martial arts fighter. She held both the WIBA flyweight and the IFBA flyweight world titles. An all-around sports girl, Reid played soccer, basketball, softball, and volleyball from fifth grade through high school. She has no amateur boxing experience but instead practiced karate and kickboxing in her early teens, winning the Arizona State Kickboxing title at 17 years old.

Baby Doll prays before and after each fight and always has her lucky teddy bear which she inherited from her paternal great grandmother. Her mother, Rose, is always at her side braiding Reid's hair prior to fights. Reid turned professional in April 2000 and won her debut versus Jo Ellen Caldwell by a unanimous decision, but lost three months later. For the next five years, she would rack up an impressive

15 wins, 5 draws, and no loss record. During this winning stretch, she challenged Germany's Regina Halmich for the WIBF flyweight title but lost by a split decision. On August 31, 2006, the Filipino American southpaw finally grabbed a world championship when she beat Stephanie "All Action" Dobbs for the WIBA flyweight title. The following year, she added another world championship belt when she defeated the taller South Korean, Shin-Hee Choi, for the IFBA flyweight title.

Plagued by injuries sustained from her mixed martial arts competitions, Reid's career took a downward trajectory and she announced retirement and marriage in 2011. While boxing, she had continued her college studies at the University of Nevada, Las Vegas (UNLV) and graduated with a degree in marketing. Inspired by her mother's passion to give back to

Newly crowned world champion Elena Reid poses with her mom, Rose, and her lucky Teddy bear
Photo credit: Mary Ann Owen

the less fortunate in the community, Baby Doll is involved in a number of non-profit organizations and hopes to one day run her own. She thrives in the values of her Filipino heritage—strong family ties, education, and Catholic faith. Reid also looks forward to savoring her favorite Filipino food—*lumpia* (spring roll) and *halo-halo* (mix-fruit in shaved ice dessert)—after her fights.

Sarah "Thrilla from Manila" Goodson (28 wins, 17 losses, 1 draw, 9 KOs)

The fourth of our fearless Filipina boxers is Philippine-born Sarah "Thrilla from Manila" Goodson. She was born Sarah Bihagan Rama on September 7th, 1973. Her Philippine hometown is Lomboy in Cebu City, which is located in the Visayan region. Goodson is the second to the oldest of eight siblings of jeepney driver Meliton Rama from Cebu City and housewife Masing Bihagan from Argao, Cebu Province. Life was very hard for the large family with her father barely making enough to feed and clothe everyone. Nonetheless, Goodson completed her elementary education and high school in Cebu and dreamed of going abroad. She immigrated to the U.S. in 1994.

Barely 5' tall, the petite Goodson, married her trainer-manager Stacy "Goodnight" Goodson in September 1999 and changed her name to Sarah Ann Goodson. They have two sons, Sergio and Sean, who are both autistic. Husband Stacy was a professional boxer with 82 pro fights in a career that lasted 12 years. They settled in Paris, Arkansas. Her boxing idols are Carina Moreno, Mike Tyson, and Manny Pacquiao. Her ring alias is "Thrilla from Manila."

Like Reid, Goodson has no amateur boxing record. She just jumped into professional boxing to earn additional income, with her husband's encouragement. She turned professional in 1999 at a time when women's professional boxing was still struggling to gain respect and attention. She admits that she got into it mainly to gain "some good money" and did not train very seriously. Most of the fight preparation was done in her front porch and living room especially during the winter. Along with her professional boxing, Goodson always had a full-time job and was a full-time mother to her two special-needs children.

Inside the ring, Goodson is a hard-hitter who thrives on her signature nasty overhand right. She is the first Filipina to win a world championship belt—the WIBF junior straw-weight title. Goodson achieved this by beating the tough-as-nails Stephanie "All Action" Dobbs via a split decision on August 8th, 2004, at Desert Diamond Casino in Tucson, Arizona. But the road to achieving a world title was not easy. Sarah debuted against Nina "The Bomb" Ahlin in August 1999 and would lose via an embarrassing first-round TKO. Her lack of training consistency resulted in nine losses.

Many prizefighters would have stopped by then but not the strong-willed Filipina from Cebu. The Thrilla from Manila finally notched her first win on May 26, 2000 by a second round TKO of Crystal Parker at the Pavilion on Logan Woods

The Thrilla from Manila gets ready for battle
Photo credit: Sarah Goodson

in Kansas City, Missouri. For the next two years, Goodson would come up with a measly four wins and three losses. She vied for the vacant IFBA minimumweight title against Canadian "Vicious" Vaia Zaganas and succumbed by TKO.

From 2002-2004, the Thrilla from Manila chalked up five wins, two losses, and a draw, which entitled her to a title shot in August 2004—finally prevailing five years after turning pro. After winning the WIBF junior straw-weight title that year, Goodson gained a boxing champion's confidence and decided to invest in a more permanent training facility as well as a consistent training routine. It paid off in terms of wins—16 in all—and just two defeats. Goodson has not fought since her last losing battle versus Hungary's Krisztina "Baby" Belinszky for the Global Boxing Union female minimumweight title.

11

People's Champ

"Nasa Diyos ang awa, nasa tao ang gawa."
(Mercy resides in God; deeds are in men.)

These days the rise of the best pound-for-pound boxer in the world would only be possible with the essential "three Ps" outside the square ring: purse, promoter, and pay-per-view. The last one underscores that fame and glory in any sport are products of both hard work in the gym and the power of the media.

In the past, Filipino prizefighters such as Pancho Villa, Ceferino Garcia, and the Magnificent Four (Little Pancho, Small Montana, Little Dado, and Speedy Dado) were literally judged by the media that propped them up as sports stars. "Newspaper decisions" were common: a pool of ringside newspaper reporters, after a "no decision contest," simply agreed among themselves who they would declare as the winner.

These boxers' stellar ring records spoke for themselves. Nowadays, however, there wouldn't be any internationally recognizable boxing stars, like Foreman, Tyson, Holyfield, De La Hoya, Mayweather, or Pacquiao, without newspapers, magazines, the internet, and radio. Topping them all is the pay-per-view (PPV) channel's relentless 24/7 bombardment on literally everything and anything about the boxer's lives inside and outside the ring. PPV has become so influential that people make a big deal of the pugilists, not the world titles that are at stake. Moreover, the agreed purse is only a fraction of what a boxer will receive since pay-per-view revenues could easily reach hundreds of millions of dollars. For instance, the 2007 De La Hoya vs. Mayweather fight brought in a record 2.4 million buys for HBO. Moreover, PPV has been good for the withering interest in boxing globally.

Manny "Pacman" Pacquiao is the last of the outstanding sluggers we cover in this book because he is not just an eight-division world champ, he has become a PPV and media mega-star. He is much a product of the 21st century media as his eight-week training sessions in Baguio City, north of Manila and at the Wild Card Gym in Los Angeles. The Filipino pugilist has become the single most internationally recognizable Philippine brand. We see him on a Nike billboard on the main shopping district in San Francisco's Union Square as well as on cereal boxes. Millions of people watch his fights whether it is a title shot or not. That is why his running PPV tally has gotten out of control:

- December 6, 2008, Manny Pacquiao vs. Oscar De La Hoya: 1.25 million buys
- May 2, 2009, Manny Pacquiao vs. Ricky Hatton: 850,000 buys
- November 14, 2009, Manny Pacquiao vs. Miguel Cotto: 1.25 million buys
- March 13, 2010, Manny Pacquiao vs. Joshua Clottey: 700,000 buys
- November 13, 2010, Manny Pacquiao vs. Antonio Margarito: 1.15 million buys
- May 7, 2011, Manny Pacquiao vs. Shane Mosley: 1.3 million buys

The media owns him and he owns the media. Pacquiao was named "Fighter of the Decade" by the Boxing Writers Association of America and "Athlete of the Decade" by the Philippine Sportswriters Association. By the end of the decade, he was rated as the world's best boxer by high-profile and influential 24/7 internet media outlets such as *The Ring*, BoxRec.com, *Sports Illustrated*, ESPN, NBC Sports, Yahoo! Sports, and *Sporting Life*. He has appeared in *Time Magazine*'s "100 Most Influential People" list as well as *Forbes Magazine* "World's Highest-Paid Athletes" list.

This international popularity is topped by the close to a hundred million Filipinos in the Philippines and globally who put their lives on hold to watch his fights and beam with pride.

During his bouts, there is an unofficial ceasefire between the security forces and rebels in conflict areas. The crime rate also drops to virtually zero.

His humble beginnings

Everywhere we go in the world, from Durban, South Africa, to Tijuana, Mexico, from New York to San Francisco, one of the most commonly asked questions thrown at us when they find out we are Filipino is: Do you know Pacquiao? Then they start hitting the air with their fist.

Despite his overwhelming popularity, Pacquiao does not want to be known as a media megastar. He would rather be recognized as the People's Champ.

How did Pacquiao get to his pedestal so quickly? He certainly does not have Paris Hilton's headstart in terms of name recognition and wealth. But he is catching up. Unlike Hilton, Pacman Pacquiao had very humble beginnings that has parallels to the first prizefighter we discussed in this book, Pancho Villa.

Emmanuel Dapidran Pacquiao, nicknamed "Manny," was born on December 17, 1978 in the municipality of Kibawe in the province of Bukidnon, Philippines. He is the fourth among the six children raised by his mother, Dionesia Dapidran-Pacquiao. She had two children from a first relationship and four with Pacquiao's father, Rosalio. Dionisia and Rosalio Pacquaio separated when Manny was in the sixth grade. [If you recall, Pancho Villa's father abandoned his family too.]

Manny Pacquiao eventually dropped out of high school due to extreme poverty so he sold cigarettes and doughnuts in the streets to help his mother earn some money. There were many street kids doing the same thing thus protecting one's territory was important. This was where Manny excelled. He downed the big bullies and always came to the rescue of the smaller kids.

The family moved to the bigger city of General Santos in the province of South Cotabato where Pacquiao would play street basketball and fight bouts for a few dollars every Sunday. At 14, he ran away from home and took the inter-island ferry to join some of his close boxing buddies in the Philippine capital city of Manila.

At first, Pacquaio missed his family and was overwhelmed by the big city, but he eventually found his bearings and worked as a day laborer for construction jobs. Life was hard. There were days when he slept on cardboard boxes on the city streets. [Pancho Villa also left his family and survived the harsh metropolis in similar fashion.] With his hands wrapped in towel rags, the barefoot Pacquiao would box on the street alleys and corners.

As fate would have it, the young Pacquiao found his way to the dingy L&M Gym on Paquita Street in Sampaloc, one of the busiest neighborhoods in Manila. He watched and trained as hard as the older boxers. In his off days, he and his friends spent hours watching videos of Larry Holmes, Joe Frazier and George Foreman, aside from playing lots of pick-up basketball on the streets. Basketball was an integral part of his and many Filipino boxers' cross-training.

Two events nudged Pacquiao to eventually turn professional: first, he had already accumulated more than 60 amateur contests, winning more than 95 percent of them and second, he aspired to be on "Blow-by-Blow," a boxing show on Vintage Sports, the equivalent of ESPN in the Philippines.

Even as a kid in General Santos City, Pacquaio already had his eye on TV sports stardom and so he became a pro before he turned 17 in December 1994. At that time, he was barely 5' tall and weighed less than 100 pounds. He looked very lean but had a mean build, with solid abdominals and toned muscles. The years of hard physical labor in the streets of General Santos and Manila, along with his strenuous gym workouts and his basketball and running had developed his core strength, and more importantly, his stamina and agility.

Pacquiao's professional debut was on January 22, 1995 against Edmund "Enting" Ignacio in the province of Mindoro Occidental, in central Philippines. He placed weights in his pocket to make the 105-pound minimum weight. At the end of the day, he had his first career victory.

Pacquiao would run up 10 straights wins before being knocked out by Rustico Torrecampo in February 1996. Undeterred, the 18-year-old trained even harder and managed a string of eight wins, mostly by early-round TKOs and KOs. By this time, the southpaw was receiving more and more attention from "Blow-by-Blow" broadcasters who were fond of commenting on his raw but relentless punching style.

On the June 26, 1997 edition of the show, Pacquiao fought Thailand's Chokchai Chockvivat (34-2-0 record) for the Orient and Pacific Boxing Federation (OPBF) flyweight title. After heavy exchanges during the early rounds, he managed to find an opening in the fifth and knocked out the more experienced defending champion. Pacquiao had won his first international title.

At his first title defense before his hometown fans in South Cotabato, Pacquiao KO'd fellow southpaw Panomdej Ohyuthanakorn in the first round. Five months later, he flew to Japan and repeated the feat with another first-round KO of challenger Shin Terao before a shocked crowd at Tokyo's Korakuen Hall. Newspaper write-ups, as well as radio and TV reports on his victories trickled in, supplementing his Vintage Sports coverage. The word started to get around that there is a new surging star in Philippine boxing—and his charming smile was winning the hearts of the people.

For God, country and the Filipino people

Besides being called "Manny" by family and those close to him, and the "People's Champ" by politicos, the public and the media, Pacquiao has picked up a number of other monikers, including "Pacman," "The Destroyer," "The Mexicutioner," "*Pambansang Kamao*" (National Fist) and "The Fighting Congressman."

Pacquiao believes in God's grace but knows that it needs to be supplemented by human action. A devout Catholic, Pacquiao kneels down at his corner and thanks God immediately after each fight (win or lose) and dedicates every win to his beloved country and people. This is the higher cause that drives the planet's first eight-division world champion and the first boxer in history to win ten world titles. Obviously that is why God, country, and the Filipino people are the recurring themes of his favorite fight songs: "*Para Sa'yo Ang Laban na 'To*" (This Fight is for You) and "*Laban Nating Lahat Ito*" (This is Our Fight). He sang and recorded them himself. Not surprisingly, millions of followers use the People's champion's songs as their inspirational ring tones on their cell phones.

Filipinos love their world champions so they celebrated when Pacquiao conquered his first world division title by winning the WBC flyweight title in December 1998 versus Chatchai Sasakul. His opponent was highly favored with an impressive 33-1-0 record going into the fight. Pacquiao however knocked out the rising Thai prizefighter in the eighth round before a shocked hometown crowd in Phuttamonthon, Thailand. He had become a sensation beyond the "Blow-by-Blow" TV show. Sadly though, he would lose the WBC flyweight title to Sasakul's compatriot, Medgoen "3K Battery" Singsurat, via a third round knockout a year later. Some thought that that was the end of his rise to fame. After all, the Philippines has had many world boxing champions who had short-lived reigns. So what's different with this Pacquiao guy?

Determined to prove his detractors wrong, Pacquiao stepped back into the ring three months after his humiliating loss in Thailand and TKO'd his compatriot Reynante Jamili for the WBC International super bantamweight title in December 1999. It was not a world title but at least he had an international title to boost his confidence. He would defend this title five times.

As fate would have it, an offer came to his manager for Pacquiao to be a last-minute replacement for the IBF super bantamweight title match against former champion Lehlohonolo "Hands of Stone" Ledwaba at the MGM Grand in June 2001. Pacquiao partnered with a new trainer, the veteran Freddie Roach, and prepared hard with him at his Wild Card Gym in Los Angeles, California.

Pacquiao listens respectfully to his trainer and mentor, Freddie Roach

Photo credit: Ronnie Lu

Under Roach's tutelage, Pacquiao sharpened his technique and style. And it paid off when he stopped the South African via a sixth round TKO. He was once again a world champion as he picked up his second division title win. The boxing media and Philippine public began to take him more seriously when he successfully defended the IBF title four times.

But the fight that would define Pacquiao's career and expand his international media coverage and fan base was his bout against Marco Antonio Barrera in November 2003. Before the evening ended, he had defeated Mexico's "Baby Faced Assassin" and had gained *The Ring* Featherweight World title belt with an eleventh round TKO at the Alamodome in San Antonio, Texas. With this title, Pacquiao also became the first Filipino and the first Asian to become a three-division world champion, surpassing many great Philippine and Asian boxers who came before him and tried. Six months later, he challenged Juan Manuel "Dinamita" Márquez for his two world titles but the fight ended up in a controversial draw, even though Pacquiao had downed Marquez three times in the first round. The global media were now eager to see his exciting ring battles.

In March 2005, Pacquiao moved up to the super featherweight division and challenged another Mexican great, the three-division world champion Érik "El Terrible" Morales for the vacant WBC International and IBA Super Featherweight titles, but lost in a unanimous decision. He was too predictable—speedy hands but lacking in footwork. It was back to the drawing board.

Pacquiao and Roach worked hard to correct these flaws. Six months later, the Filipino champ annexed the vacant WBC International super featherweight title with a win over Mexico's Hector Velazquez. He would defend this international title against five gritty Mexican challengers for three years, beating past foes—Morales, convincingly, twice and Barrera for the second time.

Pacquiao's fourth world division title was achieved via a rematch entitled "Unfinished Business" with Marquez for the WBC super featherweight title on March 15th, 2008 at the Mandalay Bay Resort and Casino in Las Vegas, Nevada. He prevailed in a split decision.

Filipinos had only began to celebrate yet another record when Pacquiao won his fifth world division title three months later in a tense slugfest against fellow southpaw David "Dangerous" Diaz which ended with a ninth round TKO and the Pacman going home with the WBC Lightweight title.

The beginning of Pacquiao's ascension to PPV stardom was not even a title fight, but the contest had an atmosphere equivalent to it since he was going in the ring against six-division world champion and founding partner of Golden Boy Promotions, Oscar de la Hoya. The "Dream Match" was held on December 6, 2008 before a crowd of 16,000 who packed the MGM Grand in Las Vegas, Nevada.

Pacquiao went into the fight already a five-division world champion, tied with boxing greats such as Thomas "The Hitman" Hearns, Sugar Ray Leonard, and the unbeaten Floyd "Pretty Boy" Mayweather, Jr. During the break between the eighth and ninth rounds, the outclassed, tired, and beaten Golden Boy decided to throw in the towel. De la Hoya announced his retirement from the ring shortly after. The fight was watched by more than one million domestic households. The gate revenue at 17 million was the second highest in boxing history.

With Pacquiao's winning trajectory, it did not take him very long to tie de la Hoya and surpass Hearns, Leonard, and Mayweather's records. In a contest billed as "The Battle of the East and West", Pacquiao jumped out of the bell with guns blazing and had Ricky "The Hitman" Hatton down twice by the first round. The end for Hatton came in the second round with a one-two punch followed by a sharp left hook which had the highly regarded challenger on his back gazing at the arena lights. The People's Champion had become the IBO light welterweight champion and had added his sixth world division title. The spectacular knockout won him *The Ring Magazine*'s "Knockout of the Year" for 2009. HBO reported more than a quarter of a million PPV buys.

The People's Champ became a class of his own with world division titles #7 and #8, won between 2009 and 2011. Very few will be able to approximate these unbelievable feats. In November 2009, he beat Miguel Angel Cotto for the

WBO welterweight title and defended it successfully against the taller Ghanian Joshua Clottey. Eight months later, in another lopsided contest, Pacquiao would defeat yet another Mexican former world champion, Antonio "The Express Train" Margarito, for the vacant WBC super welterweight title. The 5'11 Margarito who came to the fight 17 pounds heavier than Pacquiao left the Cowboys Stadium with a badly swollen face and a large cut beneath the right eye.

On May 7, 2011, the People's Champ blasted Shane "Sugar" Mosley with his trademark speedy but powerful punches, downing the American challenger in the third round. After 12 rounds, Pacquiao prevailed via unanimous decision. The gate receipts at the MGM Grand in Las Vegas totaled close to nine million dollars from more than 15,000 tickets, the 14th-highest attendance revenue in Nevada's boxing history. The domestic PPV buys added another 1.3 million buys worth $75 million. In addition to Pacquiao's hard-to-break boxing accomplishments, the four million PPV buys for his last six fights certainly went a long way toward helping pump up America's sagging economy.

The People's Champ has so far managed to escape the personal, professional, and business management issues that have plagued some of the pugilists in this book. He has had drinking and fidelity issues but has finessed them over the years. Paquiao has also been taken advantage of by greedy promoters early on in his career but has recovered and learned well from these setbacks. He and his wife, Jinkee, have also

Pacquiao and Shane Mosley at the pre-fight weigh in
Photo credit: Victor Sy

become business savvy, investing in business ventures in Manila and General Santos City as well as taking advantage of his popularity to endorse Philippine and American products, from San Miguel Beer to Nike shoes.

Most of all, the People's Champ is giving back to community and social justice causes. Pacquiao was elected to the Philippine Congress in May 2010. He faces the toughest battle of his life, representing, Sarangani, one of the most under-developed provinces in the Philippines. Only time will tell what his real legacy will be.

References

Afable, Jorge, editor, (1972). *Philippine Sports Greats* (Mandaluyong: Man Publishing).

Alinea, Eddie (2010). "Pancho Villa: Greatest Flyweight of 20th Century" PhilBoxing.com. June 23, 2010.

Alinea, Eddie (2010). "Remembering Flash Elorde". Philboxing.com. March 24, 2011.

Bacho, Peter (1997). *Dark Blue Suit and Other Stories*. Seattle: University of Washington.

Bernardo, Fernando A. (2000). *Silent Storms: Inspiring Lives of 101 Great Filipinos* (Pasig: Anvil Publishing)

Borrinaga, Rolando O. (1994). "Where is Ceferino Garcia?" *Philippine Daily Inquirer*, November 27 issue.

boxrec.com

Dettloff, William (2011). "The 10 Greatest Filipino-Fighters of all-Time." *The Ring*, August 2011 issue.

España-Maram, Linda (2006). *Creating Masculinity in Los Angeles's Little Manila: Working-Class Filipinos and Popular Culture, 1920s-1950s*. New York: Columbia University Press.

filipinoboxingjournal.com

Henson, Joaquin (2010). "Garcia snubbed by boxing body." *The Philippine Star*, July 1, 2010 issue.

International Boxing Research Organization

Interview with Ana Julaton, boxer, July 16, 2011.

Interview with Ben Villaflor, boxer, June 11, 2011.

Interview with Dodie Boy Peñalosa, July 13, 2011.

Interview with Elena Reid, August 16, 2011

Interview with Glen Donaire, July 6, 2011.

Interview with Gretchen Abaniel, August 17, 2011

Interview with Juan Martin Bai Elorde, May 2005.

Interview with Raymundo Fortaleza, May 31, 2011

Interview with Sarah Goodson, boxer, August 15, 2011

Interviews with Luisito Espinosa, Fall 2006-Fall 2007.

Interviews with Nonito Donaire Sr., May 31, 2011 and June 28, 2011.

Mills, Norris C. (1925). "Filipino Boxing Invasion Coming," *The Ring*. September 1925 issue, page 17.

Nathanielsz, Ronnie (2008). "Remembering 'Flash' Elorde", Philboxing.com, January 3, 2008.

Pacquiao, Manny and James, Timothy (2010). *Pacman: My Story of Hope, Resilience, and Never-Say-Never Determination*. Los Angeles, CA: Dunham Books.

Pamintuan, Carlo (2008). "Gerry Penalosa–Beating the Boxing Odds". eastsideboxing.com. March 29, 2008 issue.

Pasquil, Corky and and Edralin, Agrafino (1994). "The Great Pinoy Boxing Era". Video documentary.

Poole, Gary Andrew (2010). *PacMan: Behind the Scenes with Manny Pacquiao--the Greatest Pound-for-Pound Fighter in the World*. Cambridge, MA: Da Capo Press.

Samson, Johnny (1926). "History of Boxing in the Philippines." In DeWitt Van Court, *The Making of Champions in California*. Los Angeles: Premier Printing.

Selected news clippings from *Tacoma News Tribune, New York Times, Chicago Tribune, Philadelphia Record, Philippine Star, Philippine Daily Inquirer, Philippine Free Press, Manila Bulletin, Toronto Star, Philippine Herald, Mirror Magazine, The Ring, Knockout, Referee, Los Angeles Times, United Press, Philippines Review (Los Angeles), Associated Filipino Press (Los Angeles), Filipino Pioneer (Stockton), Los Angeles Filipino Bulletin*.

Svinth, Joseph R. (2001). "The Origins of Philippines Boxing, 1899-1929." *Journal of Combative Sport*, July issue.

Trinidad, Recah (2006). *Pacific Storm: Dispatches on Pacquiao of the Philippines*. Pasig: Anvil Press.

Van, Bill (1931). "Speedy Dado is a Pancho Villa," *Knockout*. February 21, 1931 issue.

Villegas, Dennis (2006). "Pancho Villa: First Filipino World Boxing Champion" pilipinokomiks.blogspot.com (May 9, 2006).

Wiley, Mark (1994). *Filipino Martial Arts: Cabales Serrada Escrima*. Rutland: Tuttle Publishing.

www.abs-cbnnews.com, "Filipino ex-boxing world champ hurt in stabbing", February 14, 2008 issue

Zonio, Aquiles (2005). "Ex-world boxing champ knocked out in GenSan," *Philippine Daily Inquirer*, March 21, 2005 issue.

A Big "Thank You" to the following:

- The University of San Francisco (USF)'s Maria Elena Yuchengco Endowment and College of Arts and Sciences for the generous financial support;

- Our colleagues at the USF Yuchengco Philippine Studies Program, Asian Studies Program, Politics Department, Asian American Studies Program, and the Center for the Pacific Rim, for their encouragement, most especially Dean Marcelo Camperi;

- The USF Boxing Club and our Philippine boxing students for their inspiration;

- Chuck White, Director of the Koret Recreational Sports Department, for his friendship, feedback, and facilities;

- Jessica Lemaux, Asian Studies and Yuchengco Philippine Studies Program Assistant, for the swift photocopying and scanning;

- Kylah Esperanza Frazier and Katherine Bowen-Williams for the research assistance as well as Caroline Calderon, Erwin Sunga, and Marc C. Merino for the proofreading;

- International Boxing Research Organization boxing historians Tracy Callis and Tony Triem, Robert Abila, Mary Ann Owen, Nonito Donaire Sr., Rudy Asercion as well as Ronnie Lu for generously allowing us to use their photographs;

- Elise Borbon Gonzalez for the cover and interior design ideas; and

- Gemma Nemenzo, our editor, for her sharp eyes and fact-checking.

About the Authors

Joaquin Jay Gonzalez III is Associate Professor of Politics, Chair of the Asian Studies Program, and Director of the Maria Elena Yuchengco Philippine Studies Program at the University of San Francisco (USF). Dr. Gonzalez is the author of numerous books, including *Diaspora Diplomacy: Philippine Migration and its Soft Power Influences*. He has a B.A. in History and Political Science from De La Salle University (Manila), a Master of Public Administration from the University of the Philippines, and a Ph.D. in Political Science from the University of Utah. Dr. Gonzalez is a USF assistant boxing coach, certified by U.S. Amateur Boxing.

Angelo Michael F. Merino received his B.A. in Economics from San Sebastian College in Manila, Philippines and a Masters in Sport and Fitness Management from the University of San Francisco (USF). He is the head boxing coach of USF and is internationally certified and recognized by the Amateur Boxing Association of the Philippines and U.S. Amateur Boxing. Coach Angelo is an adjunct professor with the USF Yuchengco Philippine Studies and Asian Studies Programs, co-teaching with Dr. Gonzalez: "Philippine Boxing and Culture" and "Boxing and Social Justice."

CPSIA information can be obtained at www.ICGtesting.com
Printed in the USA
LVOW090908230512

282934LV00001B/44/P